Tales Of Lawyer Ramachandra Shastry

OrangeBooks Publication

1st Floor, Rajhans Arcade, Mall Road, Kohka, Bhilai, Chhattisgarh 490020

Website: **www.orangebooks.in**

© Copyright, 2024, Author

All rights reserved. No part of this book may be reproduced, stored in a retrieval system, or transmitted, in any form by any means, electronic, mechanical, magnetic, optical, chemical, manual, photocopying, recording or otherwise, without the prior written consent of its writer.

First Edition, 2024

ISBN: 978-93-6554-663-7

TALES OF LAWYER
RAMACHANDRA SHASTRY

CHAITANYA SG

OrangeBooks Publication
www.orangebooks.in

About This Novel

"Tales of Lawyer Ramachandra Shastry" is more than just a courtroom drama; it is a tribute to the indomitable spirit of truth, justice, and the human condition. Through this fiction novel, I have strived to weave together a series of gripping, thought-provoking stories that delve into the complex interplay of law, society, and morality.

The protagonist, Ramachandra Shastry, is not your conventional lawyer. He is young, ambitious, and fiercely independent, tackling cases that test his wit, determination, and compassion. As Shastry navigates the labyrinth of the legal system, the reader is drawn into a world where every case is more than just a file number— it is a story of human struggles, triumphs, and, often, redemption.

In this novel, we encounter Shastry as he faces challenges that go beyond the courtroom. From grappling with personal dilemmas to confronting societal prejudices, his journey is as much about understanding life as it is about interpreting the law. Each chapter introduces compelling cases that intertwine with Shastry's evolving character, showcasing his sharp legal acumen and his unwavering commitment to justice.

The novel also sheds light on the nuances of the Indian legal system, exploring legal provisions and the intricate dance of justice between the prosecution and defense. Through Shastry's experiences, the reader gains an insider's perspective into the challenges lawyers face—whether it's the struggle for resources, the burden of moral dilemmas, or the thrill of unexpected victories.

While the cases provide the adrenaline, the heart of the novel lies in its characters. Shastry is not just a lawyer but a symbol of hope for the downtrodden, a man whose sense of empathy often outweighs his desire for material success. His interactions with clients, friends, and even adversaries reveal a deeply human side to the profession, one that often goes unnoticed in the pursuit of legal victories.

Thematically, the novel explores the intersection of law and humanity. It raises poignant questions: What does justice truly mean? Can morality and law coexist harmoniously? How far can one go to uphold the principles they believe in? Through Shastry's cases and personal struggles, I hope to inspire readers to reflect on these questions while being thoroughly entertained by the gripping narrative.

As a practicing lawyer from Bengaluru since 2008, I have drawn inspiration from real-life experiences to infuse authenticity into the novel. Yet, the stories are not just about the law—they are about the people behind the cases, the emotions that drive them, and the circumstances that bind them. Shastry's world is one where every case is a microcosm of the human experience, filled with triumphs, tragedies, and the eternal quest for justice.

This novel is a labor of love, and it stands as a testament to my passion for law and story-telling the intricate realities of the legal world. My hope is that readers, irrespective of their backgrounds, will find themselves captivated by Shastry's journey and take away something profound from his trials and triumphs.

Welcome to *"Tales of Lawyer Ramachandra Shastry"*.

Warm regards,

Mr. Chaitanya S.G.

Legal Disclaimer

This novel, *"Tales of Lawyer Ramachandra Shastry"*, is a work of fiction. The characters, events, locations, and dialogues depicted in this book are entirely the product of the author's imagination. Any resemblance to actual persons, living or deceased, events, or establishments is purely coincidental.

While the legal concepts and principles mentioned in this novel aims to provide a representation of courtroom proceedings and the law, they are included for narrative purposes and should not be considered as professional legal advice or a comprehensive guide to the legal system.

The author and publisher expressly disclaim any liability arising from interpretations or misinterpretations of the content within this novel. The primary intent of this work is to entertain, and any legal insights or situations depicted are fictionalized for storytelling purposes.

Readers are advised to consult qualified legal professionals for accurate and reliable legal guidance.

Contents

Chapter - I
Bhagyawanthi 1
- The Shed Of Dreams 1
- Beginning Of 2009 7
- The Shadows Of Bijapur 28
- The Bijapur Trail 37
- Memories Distilled 51
- The Art Of Inquiry 58
- Hon'ble High Court Of Karnataka At Kalburgi 62
- Court Is In Session At Bijapur 86
- Return To Bengaluru 130
- The Trial Ultimate 136

Chapter - II
Beyond The Known 155
- 2011- February Of Change 155
- At The Police Station 164
- At Shastry Law Associates 169
- The Storm Is Coming 212
- Unpacking The Law 216
- Under The July Sky- 2011 226
- Debt Repaid! 228
- At The Courthouse 253

Dedicated to my beloved parents Parvathi and Gururaj

Chapter - I
BHAGYAWANTHI

THE SHED OF DREAMS

The flickering tube light in Lawyer Ramachandra Shastry's "office" buzzed faintly as he leaned back in his rickety, second-hand swivel chair, stretching his arms after a long day of dealing with his usual clientele. His office—a renovated car shed that once housed his friend's rusted Maruti 800—had come a long way. He had put in his savings, every rupee he could scrape together, to turn it into something vaguely resembling a lawyer's workspace. Sure, the ceiling leaked when it rained, and the "reception area" was really just a plastic chair next to the door, but to Shastry, it was a palace.

To an outsider, it might have seemed more like a joke than an office. The walls, once stained with oil and grime from years of car repairs, had been painted a shade of white that seemed to be losing a slow battle against the relentless dust. His desk—a piece of wood salvaged from his uncle's old shop—stood proudly at the center of the room, its legs uneven, causing an annoying wobble that Shastry had tried to fix with folded pieces of paper. His law books were stacked high on a metal shelf, which leaned dangerously to one side, as if contemplating collapse.

The ceiling fan, mounted precariously, swayed with every rotation, threatening to come crashing down during the warmer months when it was forced into overtime. But despite all these imperfections, Shastry had a deep fondness for his office. It was, after all, *his* office—a symbol of his relentless determination to make a name for himself in the legal world.

The past eight months had been anything but smooth. After graduating with stars in his eyes, imagining himself in grand courtrooms arguing landmark cases, reality had hit him like a freight train. All the big law chambers had either turned him away or never called him back. He had once walked into a posh law firm, wearing his best (and only) suit, hoping to land a spot with one of the top senior advocates in Bengaluru.

The receptionist, a sharp-eyed woman with a permanent scowl, had taken one look at his resume and sighed, "We'll call you." She never did.

Shastry had quickly realized that his dreams of walking into a prestigious chamber and instantly becoming Nani Palkhivala were as distant as the stars. So, he had done what a young, overconfident graduate with too much pride and too little money would do: HE OPENED HIS OWN PRACTICE! He rented his friend's car shed for next to nothing, added a makeshift desk, a stack of law books, and voila! *Shastry Law Associates* was born.

The irony of it all wasn't lost on him. While his Law College classmates were busy posing in front of shiny new offices, with shiny new titles on shiny new business cards, Shastry was sitting under a leaky roof, with a nameplate that barely stayed in place because the wall was so uneven. The first time a potential client had visited him, they'd stood outside the shed, looking confused, as if they were trying to figure out whether they had come for legal advice or to get their scooter repaired.

Despite the humble beginnings, Shastry had somehow managed to attract a steady stream of clients—though, admittedly, they weren't exactly the kind of clients he had imagined in law school. Instead of corporate tycoons embroiled in billion-rupee deals or high-profile criminal cases, his office was filled with local rowdies, petty criminals, runaway couples looking to get married or disgruntled husbands looking for quick divorces.

On any given day, his reception area (read: plastic chair) would be occupied by a chain-smoking man with tattoos, or a woman who looked like she had just escaped a neighborhood brawl. Most of them came to him for one thing: bail. Over the last eight months, Shastry had good proficiency on bail applications, navigating the intricacies mostly of Sections 436, 437, and occasionally of Section 438 of the Criminal Procedure Code, 1973. He knew the procedures of filing and listing inside out. In fact, he had become so familiar with the system that the local constables had nicknamed him "Bail Raja" behind his back. At first, it bothered him. But as the months dragged on, Shastry realized that while the cases weren't glamorous, they were steady. And for a lawyer just starting out, that was enough to keep the lights on (well, the flickering tube light, at least).

Of course, "steady" didn't mean "profitable." The clients he attracted weren't exactly flush with cash. More often than not, they paid him in installments—small, laughable sums. His favorite story to tell involved a client who, after being granted bail, had thanked him profusely and handed him a plastic bag filled with *change*—all ten and five-rupee coins. "I have a policy," Shastry had joked to Shekar, one of his few remaining friends who hadn't gone off to greener pastures. "I only accept payment in denominations SMALLER than a twenty-rupee note." Ravi had laughed, though not without pity. "Shastry, maybe you should have thought this through. You know what they say—starting a law practice without a senior is like going to war without a sword. What are you going to do when your clients start paying you in *paan* and *bidi* packets?" Shastry had waved him off. "It's all part of the adventure, my friend."

Despite his upbeat attitude, life as an independent lawyer wasn't without its challenges. The ceiling, for instance, was an ongoing source of frustration. It was a miracle that it was still holding up. During the rainy season, water would drip down in a steady stream, landing directly onto his desk. On more than one occasion, Shastry had been forced to push his important legal documents aside and replace them with a bucket. One particularly stormy afternoon, just as Shastry was reviewing a client's bail application, the ceiling had decided to take things up a notch. Without warning, a small section of plaster had come crashing down onto his desk, narrowly missing his head.

"That's the universe's way of telling you to quit while you're ahead," Shekhar had joked when Shastry had called him to complain. Shastry, standing amidst the debris of his office, had simply shrugged. "Quit? This is just getting started!" The rain hadn't stopped him, and neither had the constant barrage of unsolicited advice from everyone he knew. From his landlord, Mr. Narayan, to the tea seller at the court canteen, everyone seemed to have an opinion on how Shastry should be running his practice.

"You know, Shastry," Mr. Narayan had once said while collecting the rent, "most people wouldn't rent their car sheds to a lawyer. They'd say it's bad luck. But not me! No, no, I believe in justice! I believe in helping young people. Now, about that leaking ceiling..." Shastry had simply nodded along, knowing full well that the ceiling wasn't going to get fixed anytime soon. Mr. Narayan had been "meaning to fix it" for the past five months. But who was Shastry to argue? After all, he was getting the place for a steal, and beggars couldn't be choosers.

If the office wasn't enough of a challenge, there was always the matter of keeping up with the expenses. Running a law practice was, it turned out, not cheap. And while Shastry had somehow managed to scrape together enough money to cover his rent, utilities, and the occasional tube light replacement, there was always one cost he could never quite get ahead of: his tab at the court canteen. The canteen, a dingy little corner of the courthouse that served watery tea and stale biscuits, had become Shastry's second home. Most days, he couldn't afford a proper lunch, so he'd sit in the canteen nursing a cup of tea for as long as possible, hoping it would fill him up until dinner. The canteen owner, Ramesh, had been surprisingly generous, allowing Shastry to run up a tab that was now reaching comical proportions.

"Shastry sir, if you don't pay this month's bill, I'll have to start charging you interest," Ramesh would say with a grin every time Shastry ordered another round of biscuits on credit. "I'm good for it," Shastry would reply with a wave, as if he were a high-rolling lawyer with clients lined up at the door. "Just waiting on a big case to come through."

But the truth was, the "big case" was just a distant dream. For now, Shastry had to make do with the rowdies, the petty criminals, and the never-ending line of bail applications.

Yet despite the leaky roof, the plastic chair "reception," and the endless teasing from his friends, Shastry remained undeterred. There was a part of him that loved the chaos, the unpredictability of it all. Each day was a new adventure, and while his clients may not have been the high-profile criminals he had once imagined, they were *his* clients. And that meant something. In his quieter moments, usually late at night when the flickering tube light was the only source of illumination, Shastry would sit back lighting his cigarette in his rickety chair and imagine the future. One day, he would argue in front of the High Court, his name would appear on the daily cause list of "THE HONORABLE HIGH COURT OF KARNATAKA AT BENGALURU!!", and his office wouldn't be a leaky car shed—it would be a proper chamber, with a proper desk, and a proper sign out front.

But for now, Shastry was content. Content to be the lawyer who operated out of a car shed, who took on cases no one else wanted, and who always—always—kept his sense of humor intact. Because if there was one thing Shastry knew, it was that a sense of humor was the best weapon he could have when the ceiling was leaking, the clients were broke, and the tea and cigarette was always on credit.

BEGINNING OF 2009

Shastry had handled several small bail matters in the last eight months, mostly dealing with local rowdies and anti-social elements who didn't exactly make for the most law-abiding citizens. Sections 436, 437, and 438 of the Criminal Procedure Code, 1973 had become his bread and butter. He had developed a certain reputation among the rougher elements of society—he was their lawyer, the man who would show up in court with barely any notice and argue their bail applications with fervor. His friends, however, never missed a chance to pull his leg.

"Ah, look who's here! The defender of rowdies, the protector of goons!" his friend Omprakash had teased him at the court canteen just that afternoon, while stuffing his face with a plate of idlis.

"Hey Shastry, when are you planning to handle a real case?" another friend, Sunil, chimed in, barely containing his laughter. "You know, like a case that doesn't involve some guy who got drunk and slapped a constable?"

Shastry, chewing on his masala dosa—which he'd ordered on credit, yet again—simply smiled, trying to take the jibes in stride. But it was hard not to feel the sting. His practice, if one could even call it that, was small, underfunded, and unglamorous. Clients came to him not because of his brilliance but because his fees were cheap, and he wouldn't judge them for being small-time crooks.

The judges weren't too impressed either. "Mr. Shastry!," one magistrate had sighed during a particularly mundane bail hearing, "maybe you should have practiced under a senior for a few years before jumping into the deep end of law practice. You seem to be struggling to stay afloat."

Shastry had nodded politely, biting his tongue. He knew they were right, but what could he do? This was the only path he had, and despite all the mockery and financial struggles, deep down, he believed this was the best beginning he could have hoped for. Every night, after his last client had left and he was alone in his tiny office, he would resolve not to quit. Not now. Not ever.

But that didn't stop the weight of reality from bearing down on him. His finances were in a disastrous state. Most days, he barely had enough money to fill petrol in his beloved Discover 125cc bike. He ate lunch at the court canteen on loan and could only dream of upgrading his office furniture, which looked like it had survived the Partition.

Yet, despite his poverty, Shastry prided himself on his appearance. He always showed up to court impeccably dressed in a crisp white shirt, polished shoes, and neatly combed hair. "A lawyer may be poor, but he should never look poor!" Shastry used to tell himself and followed it in his heart as a principle.

Shastry adjusted the collar of his white shirt—in the small mirror he'd hung on the back of his office door. He had only two white shirts and he had bought those at a street market, and while it wasn't exactly Ralph Lauren, it got the job done. He smoothed his hair, straightened hiscollar, tied his neck band and gave himself one last nod of approval. Despite his circumstances, he looked sharp. In fact, he took great pride in always looking his best, even though his pockets barely contained a rupee.

His stomach growled loudly, protesting the meager breakfast of two bananas he had wolfed down earlier on a loan from a fruit seller stationed outside his office. The loud rumble echoed through his tiny office. "Shut up," he muttered to his stomach, as if it would actually listen. Money had been tight for months. His clients—mostly local rowdies and small-time troublemakers—paid just enough to keep his practice going, but not nearly enough to let him live comfortably. His office, or as his friends jokingly called it, "Shastry's Shed of Legal Wonders," And even though it was small and rundown, it had become a little hub for all sorts of shady characters who needed legal help at bargain-basement rates. The truth was, Shastry was barely getting by. Every day felt like a balancing act, with him juggling case files, unpaid canteen bills, and gas money for his beloved Discover 125cc bike. But somehow, he kept his spirits high, knowing deep down that this was the beginning of something great.

Lunch time had arrived, and with it, Shastry's ritual visit to the court canteen. Not because the food was excellent (it was the opposite, in fact), but because he could get a meal on credit. Today's menu was particularly uninspiring: a watery sambar, a pile of overcooked rice, a pickle and a papad that looked like it had fought a losing battle with gravity.

As he sat down with his tray, he glanced at the canteen owner, Mr. Murthy, who was already frowning. "Shastry sir," Mr. Murthy began in a stern voice, leaning over the counter, "this is the seventh time you're eating on credit this month. You'll need to clear your bill, or I'm going to have to stop serving you." Shastry gave him his most charming smile. "Mr. Murthy, what kind of relationship do we have if we can't trust each other? Think of it as an investment in my future success. One day, when I'm a famous lawyer, you'll be telling people, 'Ah yes, "Advocate Shastry" used to eat in my canteen all the time!'" Mr. Murthy's frown deepened. "Famous or not, you need to pay up. I run a business, not a charity."

Shastry sighed dramatically and pointed to his half-eaten plate. "Do you really think I'm here for the cuisine? If it wasn't for your wonderful company, I'd be dining in five-star hotels. But look at me, stuck here with this... this sambar soup." Murthy rolled his eyes but couldn't suppress a grin. "Fine, fine. One more meal on credit. But no more excuses after this!" "Deal!" Shastry replied, winking. "Now if you'll excuse me, I have to save the world, one bail application at a time."

After lunch, Shastry made his way to his beloved bike—the rusty Discover 125, which had seen better days. The paint had chipped off in places, the left mirror was missing (courtesy of a close encounter with an auto-rickshaw), and the exhaust had a peculiar habit of making a noise that resembled a dying cow. But to Shastry, it was his freedom, his pride and joy, even if it guzzled petrol like a thirsty elephant.

Today, however, there was a problem. The fuel gauge hovered dangerously close to empty, and Shastry's wallet was emptier still. He opened it with a flick, hoping against hope that a rogue 50-rupee note had magically appeared inside.

Nope. Just an old ATM receipt, a crumpled visiting card from a client who had never paid, and—wait, what was this? A 20-rupee note! "Ah, the gods are kind!" Shastry declared to no one in particular, holding the note up like it was a treasure.

He headed to the nearest petrol station, where he was greeted by the attendant with a slightly bemused expression. "Sir, how much petrol do you need?" the attendant asked. Shastry handed over the 20-rupees with great ceremony. "Just give me... exactly this much."

The attendant stared at the note, then at Shastry, then back at the note. "Sir, this will give you barely a few drops. You won't even make it out of the station." Shastry sighed and leaned in conspiratorially. "Do you think you could push me a little distance if it comes to that?" The attendant chuckled and filled his tank with the tiny amount of petrol the 20 rupee note allowed. "Good luck, sir." "Thanks," Shastry replied, mounting his bike. "I'll need it."

Back in his office, Shastry was reviewing a case file when his usual clientele began trickling in. Today, it was a group of local rowdies, led by Raju Anna, a short man with a thick mustache and an equally thick accent. Raju was known for getting into brawls, but somehow always managing to dodge serious charges—thanks, in no small part, to Shastry's timely legal assistance.

"Shastry sir!" Raju Anna boomed as he entered the office, slapping Shastry on the back like they were long-lost brothers. "We have a small problem. Need a quick bail." Shastry raised an eyebrow. "Another fight, Raju Anna? Didn't I just get you bail last week?" Raju scratched his head, trying to look innocent. "Ah, that was last week. This is a new problem. A misunderstanding! They said we were creating a nuisance, but we were just celebrating a birthday."

Shastry sighed. "Celebrating with your fists, I'm sure." Raju laughed, unfazed. "You know us, Shastry sir! We're good boys at heart. But the police... they never understand." Shastry gave a resigned nod, pulling out a vakalath form. "Alright, let's see what we can do. But this time, try not to turn the birthday cake into a weapon, okay?" Raju grinned, showing off his gold tooth. "Shastry sir, you're the best! We'll make sure to keep things peaceful. At least until the next birthday." As the group left, Shastry slumped back into his chair. "I'm not a lawyer," he muttered to himself. "I'm a glorified babysitter."

As the sun set, casting long shadows across his tiny office, Shastry closed his files and leaned back in his chair. His stomach growled again, reminding him that he hadn't eaten since the sambar soup debacle earlier that day. His pockets were empty, his clients paid in pennies, and his bike was running on fumes. But despite everything, he smiled. This was his journey. He was living the life of a lawyer, even if it was far from the glamorous dream he had imagined in Law College. Sure, his friends mocked him for starting his own practice without a senior's guidance, and sure, the judges occasionally scolded him for his inexperience, but deep down, Shastry knew this was just the beginning. "Rome wasn't built in a day," he whispered to himself. "And neither was Shastry Law Associates."

He turned off the lights, locked up his office, and walked over to his bike, giving it an affectionate pat. "Don't worry, my friend. One day, we'll have enough petrol to ride without fear." With a last glance at the sky, Shastry rode off into the night, the dying cow-like noise of his bike following him as he disappeared down the road as the day ended. The world may not have known it yet, but Ramachandra Shastry was on his way even if that involved eating on credit and paying for petrol with 20-rupees.

Ramachandra Shastry sitting in his office the next day morning, was deep in thought, furiously scribbling notes for Raju Annas upcoming bail hearing, when his phone buzzed next to him. He glanced at it, and his heart leaped momentarily. Could it be a new client? Was this finally the break he'd been waiting for? He grabbed the phone with excitement, only to be greeted by a familiar, depressing message:

"Low balance! Recharge immediately to continue using your services!"

Shastry groaned, tossing the phone back onto the desk. His phone had been stuck in this limbo for days now, a silent companion, only capable of sending him daily reminders of his financial situation. The last recharge he had done was during Diwali, and now even that lifeline was gone. "Great," he muttered, rubbing his temples. "A lawyer with no balance... just another day in the life of Ramachandra Shastry."

Shastry knew he needed his phone. In a world where even the rowdiest of rowdies expected their lawyer to be "reachable at all times," not having an active mobile connection was a potential disaster. The only problem was, recharging cost money—money that Shastry, as always, didn't have. The previous week, he had tried to get his phone recharged by the local canteen-shopkeeper, Ramesh, on credit. Ramesh was not exactly a fan of giving anyone a free pass—especially not a struggling lawyer who'd already borrowed enough snacks and soda to last a lifetime.

"Shastry, saar," Ramesh had said with a patronizing smile, "I've given you credit for tea, cigarette, chips, cold drinks, biscuits... but a phone recharge? I'm not running a telecom company here!"

"Ramesh, you don't understand!" Shastry had pleaded. "How will my clients reach me? I'm their lawyer, their savior! What if I miss an important call and someone goes to jail because of it?"

Ramesh, unimpressed, had simply pointed to a sign behind the counter: No Credit for Mobile Recharges. Shastry had left, dejected, hoping he could survive on incoming calls for a while longer. The worst part was that he had even tried begging a few friends to recharge his phone, only to be met with sarcastic comments about his "booming practice."

"Shastry!" Omprakash had laughed over the phone, "I think I've given you more mobile recharges than you've won cases! You should start representing me in court soon—I'll need to recover my losses."

As if things couldn't get worse, a familiar knock echoed from the door of his office—the knock he dreaded more than anything. It was the unmistakable rhythm of his landlord, Mr. Narayan, who had the patience of a saint but the persistence of a bill collector. Shastry sighed and opened the door. There stood Mr. Narayan, his arms crossed, his eyes gleaming with that mix of disappointment and amusement he always wore when visiting his "lawyer tenant."

"Ah, Shastry," Mr. Narayan said with a broad grin, "how's the legal empire coming along?" Shastry forced a smile. "Going well, sir, going well. You know, building a practice takes time." Mr. Narayan stepped inside, shaking his head. "Building a practice? Ha! You've been 'building' for eight months, and all I've seen you build is a stack of unpaid rent slips!" Shastry winced. He knew this was coming. Mr. Narayan never failed to bring up the rent during these little "chats."

"About that, sir—"

"Now, now, Shastry," Narayan interrupted, raising a finger. "I'm a patient man. A good man, even. In fact, if I weren't such a generous soul, where would you be today, huh? You know what people say— 'Don't rent to lawyers.' But not me! I, Narayan, opened my heart and my car shed to you! No one else in this neighborhood would have done that!" Shastry nodded, his head hanging slightly. He had heard this speech at least twenty times now. "You know," Narayan continued, his voice growing dramatic, "I turned down a shopkeeper for this space. A shopkeeper! He would've paid rent on time, every month, no delays. And yet, who did I choose? You! A lawyer! Because I believed in justice, Shastry. I believed in the law!"

Shastry struggled to keep a straight face. It wasn't that Narayan was wrong—he was actually very kind for allowing him to stay so long without kicking him out—but the sheer drama with which Narayan told this story every time was becoming comical.

"You're right, Mr. Narayan," Shastry replied, his voice soft. "I've been lucky to have you as my landlord." Narayan's face softened, but his tone remained firm. "But luck doesn't pay the rent, Shastry. You owe me three months now. Three! If this were anyone else's shed, you'd be practicing law from under a tree!"

Shastry cringed. "I know, I know. Just give me a little more time. I have some new cases coming in, and—" Narayan cut him off with a wave of his hand. "Every month, its 'new cases coming in.' Look, Shastry, I'm not an unreasonable man. I'll give you another month, but after that..." He trailed off ominously. Shastry nodded solemnly. "Thank you, sir. I'll get the money."

Narayan sighed deeply. "One more month, Shastry. Remember, I could've rented this place to a man selling Masala Vade!, but no. I went with the lawyer. And what do I get? Not Vade!, but no rent and a pile of legal papers." With that, Mr. Narayan walked out, leaving Shastry to collapse into his chair. He had heard the speech before, but this time the weight of it felt heavier.

The afternoon passed slowly. Shastry sat in his office, staring at his silent phone, wondering how he had gotten into this mess. His only hope for survival was to handle more cases, but even that was becoming difficult with a phone that could only receive missed call alerts. A loud ding suddenly filled the room. Shastry perked up and grabbed his phone, hoping someone had finally called with a life-changing case. But instead, it was another reminder:

"Your phone balance is low! Please recharge to continue using our services!"

He let out an exasperated sigh. "Even the telecom company wants me to suffer!" At that moment, his door creaked open. It was Raju Anna again, this time with an even larger entourage than before. They piled into the tiny office, filling the room with the smell of paan and cigarette smoke.

"Shastry sir!" Raju Anna boomed, sitting on the edge of Shastry's desk as if he owned the place. "We have another small issue. Another fight, but this time, it's not our fault." Shastry raised an eyebrow. "When is it ever your fault, Raju Anna?" Raju grinned. "Ah, you know how it is. These things just happen. A few punches here, a few kicks there, and suddenly the police are all over us. But don't worry, it's nothing serious. Just need bail. Again."

Shastry sighed and reached for his pen. As much as he wanted to focus on larger, more prestigious cases, Raju and his gang were his bread and butter. Literally. "Alright, I'll handle it," Shastry said. "But we need to talk about my fee." Raju's grin faded. "Oh, come on, Shastry sir. You're like family now. Family doesn't charge family, right?"

Shastry leaned back in his chair, crossing his arms. "Family also doesn't have a phone with no balance and a landlord threatening to kick them out." Raju chuckled nervously. "Alright, alright, we'll pay you, don't worry."

As Raju Anna and his entourage left, Shastry couldn't help but smile. Maybe his phone would get recharged after all. Maybe, just maybe, things were starting to look up. But then, of course, his stomach growled loudly, reminding him that it was time to eat again. He looked over at the growing pile of IOUs from the court canteen. "Ah well," he muttered to himself. "At least I have sambar soup to look forward to."

That evening, as the sun set behind the trees, Shastry stood outside his office, looking up at the sky. He was stillbroke, still eating on credit, and still behind on rent. But he wasn't defeated. Far from it. As he mounted his Discover 125cc, giving the fuel tank an affectionate pat, he whispered, "We're still in the race, old friend and as he sped off into the night, his bike sputtering and coughing, Shastry couldn't help but laugh at the absurdity of it all. Because in his heart, he knew one thing: this was only the beginning of his journey. And one day, the world.

It was a typical morning in the court of Judge Raghunath—a man whose temper was as unpredictable as a spinning roulette wheel. Shastry, standing outside Courtroom No. 4, took a deep breath and straightened his white shirt. He had a big day ahead. The infamous Raju Anna, along with his merry gang of small-time troublemakers, was depending on him once again for bail. The charges this time? Public nuisance and brawling. Shastry had prepared his arguments, crafted every word with care, and felt confident.

That is, until the court clerk gave him a warning as he entered. "Be careful, Shastry sir. Judge sir is in a foul mood today. I heard he had an issue with his breakfast. His wife didn't prepare his favorite idlis this morning, and his shirt wasn't ironed properly. He's been fuming since he arrived." Shastry froze for a second, clutching his case files. "Breakfast? You mean... I'm about to argue a bail application while the judge is HANGRY?" The clerk nodded solemnly, as though announcing the coming of a storm.

Shastry gave a half-hearted smile and walked into the courtroom. He had faced tough judges before, but nothing quite as scary as a judge who hadn't been fed properly. Inside the courtroom, Raju Anna and his gang sat at the back, looking unusually nervous. They were used to confrontations, but even they knew that facing an angry judge was a whole different ball game. Shastry walked up to the front, greeted the Judge with a nod, and prepared to argue his case.

Judge Raghunath sat on the bench, frowning so hard it looked like his face might split in two. He glanced at Shastry with the look of a man who had woken up on the wrong side of the bed and had been pushed off it again by his dog. His judge's robes were immaculate, but his mood clearly wasn't.

Shastry cleared his throat and began, "Your Honor, I—"

"Mr. Shastry," Judge Raghunath interrupted, his voice laced with irritation, "you're late." Shastry blinked. He wasn't late. In fact, he was five minutes early, but now was definitely not the time to argue with a hungry judge.

"Apologies, Your Honor," Shastry said, bowing his head slightly. "I was just reviewing my notes to ensure I have all the documents needed to argue!"

The judge didn't seem placated. "Reviewing notes? You waste too much time with notes. Time! That's what I don't have, Mr. Shastry. Unlike you, I have a docket full of cases, and I can't spend the entire day waiting for you to make your point." Shastry, sensing the impending storm, stayed calm. He took a deep breath and said, "Of course, Your Honor. I'll keep it brief." The judge scoffed, clearly not interested in being briefed on anything. "You better. Now, let's hear this bail application of yours. But I warn you, Shastry, don't test my patience today. I've had quite a morning."

From the corner of his eye, Shastry saw Raju Anna nervously twisting his gold bracelet, his face turning pale. Great, Shastry thought, not only do I have to handle an irritable judge, but I also have to make sure Raju Anna doesn't faint.

"Your Honor," Shastry began slowly, choosing his words carefully. "My client, Raju Anna, has been accused of public nuisance and a minor altercation. However, I would like to point out that no serious harm was done—"

The judge banged his gavel, cutting him off again. "Harm? You think I care about harm? This court is clogged with cases of rowdies and thugs! Do you think the people of this country can live in peace with men like your client out on the streets, causing trouble?"

Raju Anna visibly flinched at being called a thug, but Shastry remained composed. He had to tread lightly now, or the entire case would be over even before it started.

"Your Honor," Shastry continued his voice calm and respectful, "I understand the court's frustration. There are indeed many cases that involve disturbances of peace. But I assure you, my client is a man who understands the consequences of his actions and is an innocent who has not caused any disturbance as alleged."

"Innocent?" The judge leaned forward, glaring at Shastry. "His innocence won't bring peace back to the streets.

What's stopping him from repeating his actions the moment he's out on bail?"

Shastry smiled softly, the kind of smile you give when you're about to deliver a blow that the other person doesn't see coming. "Your Honor, with all due respect, my client has been falsely accused in this case and is willing to provide an undertaking to the court that no such disturbance will occur again." The judge snorted. "An Undertaking? What am I supposed to do with that? Frame it and hang it on the wall?"

Shastry, unfazed, leaned in slightly and lowered his voice. "Your Honor, I would never insult this court by suggesting something as trivial as a mere piece of paper. Please look closely at the FIR. The prosecution has miserably failed to provide any cogent and prima facie material before this Hon'ble Court which would attribute the alleged crime to my clients. There are no eye witnesses, no incriminating articles have been seized from my clients and the complaint party had an earlier grudge against them. With an intention to put them behind bars, he has colluded with the police and has successfully managed to get the FIR registered. The punishment for committing such crime is not punishable with death or life imprisonment and as such it would not cause unjust if the bail is granted. My Clients are ready to abide by any conditions imposed by this Hon'ble court and shall enter regular appearance. They shall fully co-operate with the investigation and shall not tamper any witnesses. They are permanent residents of Bengaluru and shall furnish surety to ensure regular appearance.

There was a pause. The courtroom, which had been buzzing with murmurs, fell silent. Even the judge seemed taken aback by the boldness of Shastry's argument. Justice Raghunath stared at him, his earlier irritation now giving way to curiosity. "Mr. Shastry? That's a lot of confidence for a lawyer who represents rowdies."

Shastry smiled politely. "Your Honor, I may be young, and I may represent clients from all walks of life, but I stand by my word". There was a long silence as the judge considered Shastry's words. Finally, he leaned back in his chair, rubbing his chin thoughtfully. "Fine," Judge Raghunath said at last, "but mark my words, Shastry. If your client so much as sneezes in public, this court will not be so lenient next time." Shastry nodded, his smile widening just a bit. "I am grateful for the court's faith, Your Honor." With that, the judge slammed his gavel down. "Bail granted!"

As soon as the judge left the courtroom, Raju Anna practically leapt from his seat, rushing over to Shastry with wide eyes. "Shastry sir!" Raju whispered, his voice trembling with excitement and relief. "That judge was so angry! I thought we were done for! But you... you just stood there, calm like a stone. You... you pacified him!"

Shastry couldn't help but grin. "It's all about timing, Raju Anna. Never panic. Stay calm, even when the situation looks bad. Besides, a good lawyer never lets a judge's bad breakfast ruin his client's chances." Raju Anna looked at Shastry with newfound respect, as if he were gazing at some kind of legal wizard. "You're incredible, sir! I've never seen anything like that. The way you talked him down... like magic!" Shastry chuckled, shaking his head. "Not magic, Raju Anna. Just a little patience—and maybe a pinch of charm."

Later that evening, back at his humble car-shed-turned-office, Shastry was getting ready to call it a day when Raju Anna appeared at the door once again, but this time with a very different attitude. He looked almost sheepish as he walked in. "Shastry sir," Raju Anna began, "I know we've always... you know... bargained a bit when it came to your fee. But after today, I think it's time we show you the respect you deserve." Before Shastry could respond, Raju Anna pulled out an envelope and placed it on the desk. "There's Fifty Thousand Rupees in here, sir. It's for everything you've done for me and the boys. Consider it an advance for the next time we mess up."

Shastry blinked, stunned. He stared at the envelope, then back at Raju Anna. "Fifty... thousand?" Raju Anna grinned. "You're worth every rupee, sir. And don't worry; we'll try to stay out of trouble. At least for a while." Shastry couldn't suppress the smile that spread across his face. "I appreciate this, Raju Anna. But let's try to keep you and your gang out of jail from now on, alright?" Raju nodded enthusiastically, clearly in awe of his lawyer. "Absolutely, sir! You've got our word."

As Raju Anna left the office, Shastry sat down at his desk, staring at the envelope in disbelief. He had just pacified an irritable judge, won the case, and now he had enough money to pay his overdue rent, settle his canteen bills, and—dare he say it—recharge his phone. With a contented sigh, Shastry leaned back in his chair and looked up at the ceiling. "Not bad for a day's work," he said to himself, grinning like a man who had just won the lottery!

It was 10:30 p.m., and Shastry was just about to lock up for the night. His small desk was strewn with case files, most of which concerned petty crimes and bail applications. He had long ago stopped fantasizing about handling a high-profile case. Every time he tried, reality would laugh in his face. Just as he reached for the door, there was a knock. Who could possibly be visiting at this hour? Shastry thought. It had been a long day, and he wasn't in the mood for late-night visitors—especially not rowdy clients needing urgent bail.

He opened the door to find a man standing there—frail, disheveled, and clearly exhausted. The man looked as though he hadn't eaten in days, his clothes wrinkled and dusty, his eyes sunken. A small rucksack hung loosely from his hand, and his skin was pale, with beads of sweat rolling down his forehead.

"Are you... are you Advocate Shastry?" the man asked, his voice trembling, as if speaking was an effort in itself.

"Yes, I'm Shastry," he replied, eyeing the man curiously. "What's the matter?"

"I've come from a long way... I traveled over 650 kilometers to meet you," the man said, his voice barely above a whisper. Shastry's interest piqued. "Come in, please." The man stumbled in, collapsing into the only client chair in the room. Shastry quickly poured him a glass of water, watching as the man gulped it down in onego! his hands shaking. "I haven't eaten," the man confessed.

"I've been looking for you. People told me youcould help. Please, you have to help me."

Shastry's heart pounded in his chest. Who was this man? What was his story? He hadn't seen a client this desperate in a long time. "What is it?" Shastry asked, his voice steady, though his mind raced. "Tell me everything calmly." The man looked up, his eyes wide with fear.

"Murder!" he whispered. "It's a Murder case." Shastry froze! The word hung in the air like a dark cloud, casting a shadow over the small office. For months, he had dreamed of handling a murder case, but now, as it was presented to him, a chill ran down his spine.

"M-murder?" Shastry stammered, his heart pounding in his chest. This was it. The moment he had been waiting for. But was he ready?

"Yes," the man whispered, his voice shaking. "My younger brothers have been accused of murder. They've arrested them, and no one will help us. I've come all this way because they told me... they told me you were the only one who could help."

Shastry swallowed hard, trying to maintain his composure. He had handled several bail applications until now, but this... this was different. A murder case! His first! His mind raced through all the legal principles he had studied. His hands trembled as he reached for his pen, trying to make notes.

"Where are your brothers now?" Shastry asked, his voice betraying a mixture of excitement and fear. "In Bijapur jail... they've remanded them in custody. Shastry took a deep breath, trying to calm the storm of emotions swirling inside him. He had to stay focused. This was his chance. His moment. "All right," Shastry said, leaning forward. "I'll help you. But I need all the details. Everything. Tell calmly while I order for some tea and biscuits". He quickly picked up his phone and called the shopkeeper, Ramesh, who had been supplying him, tea and biscuits on credit for months.

"Ramesh, can you bring some tea and snacks to theoffice? And maybe a few bananas," Shastry added, knowing that Rajappa was starving after such a long journey. Within a few minutes, Ramesh appeared with a tray of biscuits, a pot of tea, and a small bunch of bananas.Shastry smiled warmly and thanked him. "Ramesh, how much do I owe you?"

Ramesh hesitated for a moment, then cleared his throat. "Well, Shastry, sir... the total comes to about 500 rupees now." Shastry grinned and pulled out his wallet, handing over the exact amount. For the first time in weeks, he felt proud of himself. He had finally paid off his outstanding dues.

Shastry turned to Rajappa and the man nodded frantically, tears of relief filling his eyes. He began to explain the case in broken sentences, the horror of his situation spilling out in waves. Shastry listened intently, his mind already working out the strategies he would use in court.

THE SHADOWS OF BIJAPUR

The sun hung low over the arid plains of Bijapur, casting long shadows across the landscape. The land stretched for miles, barren in parts, with patches of rich black soil where the sugarcane fields thrived. Once the seat of powerful rulers, Bijapur had a history as vast and complex as the land itself.

Founded by the Chalukyas and later taken over by the Adil Shahi dynasty, Bijapur was once a glittering gem of architecture and culture. The towering Gol Gumbaz, the mausoleum of Sultan Mohammed Adil Shah, stood as a reminder of a bygone era when art, science, and politics converged in this dusty town. The city was famous for its palaces, mosques, and intricate water systems that once kept the city flourishing in the harsh Deccan heat. But the glory of the past had long faded, replaced by a harsh, unforgiving present.

The temperature in Bijapur soared during the summer, often crossing 40°C, with no respite for the people who lived in small, scattered villages. The land was dry, and water was a precious resource, fought over and rationed among the masses. The crops grown in these villages were mainly sugarcane, which required an immense amount of water, and cotton, which provided the villagers with a meager income.

One such village, deep in the heart of Bijapur, perched at about 120 km away was where Rajappa hailed from—a village so remote, its existence was almost forgotten by the government. Houses were made of either boulders or thatched roofs, and the scarcity of water, sanitation, and access to education made life a daily struggle. There were no schools for the children, no hospitals for the sick, and no roads for easy access. The villagers toiled in the sugarcane fields owned by wealthy landlords, men who treated them as no more than disposable tools.

Rajappa hailed from a tiny village under the jurisdiction of the Almel Police, in Sindagi Taluk in Bijapur. His family, like many others, worked as laborers in the sugarcane fields of a powerful landlord named Mohan. Life in the village was hard. They lacked the basic necessities—water, food, and shelter were luxuries rather than rights. Rajappa's family, consisting of his aging parents, two elder sisters, and two younger brothers, had endured years of hardship, but nothing had prepared them for the horror that was about to unfold.

It began with the brutal rape of Rajappa's elder sister by Mohan, the landlord's son. Unable to live with the shame and trauma, his sister had thrown herself into a well, ending her life before they could even seek justice. The village wept for her, but life, as it always does, moved on. However, the grief was only compounded when Rajappa's second sister, Kamalavva, was raped and assaulted by Beerappa, a close friend of Mohan. They had tried to kill her, smashing a rock on her head, but Kamalavva had miraculously escaped, bleeding and unconscious.

When she finally regained consciousness after treatment, she had lost her mind. Over the next few days, Kamalavva wandered through the village, her spirit broken, her sanity shattered. She became a ghostly figure, haunting the very fields they once worked in. Rajappa's younger brothers, Thimmappa and Shivappa, could no longer bear the weight of their family's suffering. The rage that had been simmering inside them boiled over. They hatched a plan to take revenge.

The Deccan plains stretched out for miles, barren and dry, under the relentless heat of the Bijapur sun. The land was harsh and unforgiving, much like the lives of the people who toiled on it. In the distance, sugarcane fields swayed lazily in the faint breeze, the only signs of life amidst the parched soil. Along the horizon stood the silhouettes of ancient Baobab trees, their gnarled branches reaching skyward like the twisted arms of forgotten giants. One of these trees, weathered by time and storm, stood as a silent witness to the horror that had unfolded beneath its shade.

One evening, they waited under a Baobab tree on a lonely mud road—the very road that Mohan and Beerappa traveled to visit local liquor shop. Armed with a sword strong enough to behead a sacrifice buffalo's head, they hatched a plan to ambush the two men. This road, barely more than a path carved through the land by the feet of laborers and the wheels of ox carts, was the usual route for Mohan and Beerappa on their nightly visits to the local liquor shop. The village lay several kilometers to the south, hidden from view by low hills and the vast sugarcane fields. It was a place where time seemed to stand still, where secrets could easily disappear into the dust.

It was under this ancient Baobab that Thimmappa and Shivappa had lain in wait, their hearts filled with rage and their minds set on vengeance. The sword they carried was no ordinary weapon. It was a locally forged blade, heavy and thick, designed not for battle but for ritual sacrifice. In the villages of Bijapur, these swords were revered, used during annual festivals to behead goats and buffaloes in honor of the gods. The blade, forged by the village blacksmith with crude but effective skill, had a wide, slightly curved edge, sharpened meticulously by hand until it gleamed under the sun. It was a weapon meant for death, and in the hands of Thimmappa and Shivappa, it would deliver just that.

The sword's handle was wrapped in rough, worn leather, its grip designed to withstand the blood and sweat of ritual offerings. It was heavy, so heavy that it required two hands to wield properly, but its weight was what made it so deadly. In the village, it was known simply as "Kattega," the blade of the altar. This was no tool for self-defense; it was a butcher's instrument, meant to sever heads in one clean strike.

That fateful evening, the moon hung low in the sky, casting a pale light over the landscape as the two brothers crouched in the shadows of the Baobab tree. Their breaths were steady, their minds focused. The sword, the Kattega, rested on the ground beside them, its blade cold and menacing under the moonlight.

They could hear the faint hum of the old Splendor bike, PatPati, the local term for the bikes that Mohan and Beerappa rode, growing louder as it approached along the lonely mud road. The two men were drunk, as they always were after their visits to the liquor shop, their laughter cutting through the stillness of the night.

Thimmappa and Shivappa exchanged a glance, their faces set in grim determination. This was it—the moment they had been waiting for. The PatPati rattled closer, its engine coughing and sputtering as it struggled along the uneven path. The bike's headlamp cast an eerie glow on the road ahead, illuminating the dust in its beam like ghosts rising from the earth.

As Mohan and Beerappa neared the Baobab, Thimmappa gave a barely perceptible nod. In one fluid motion, the two brothers leapt from the shadows, their movements swift and silent. The bike screeched to a halt, Mohan and Beerappa too drunk to react in time. Before they could even process what was happening, Shivappa swung the sword with the strength of a man possessed.

The Kattega sliced through the air with a deadly hiss, and in an instant, Mohan's head was severed clean from his body. It tumbled to the ground, rolling a few feet before coming to a stop in the dust. Beerappa, frozen in terror, barely had time to scream before Thimmappa swung again, this time ending his life with equal precision.

Blood poured onto the dry earth, the dark liquid soaking into the ground like a sacrifice offered to the very land that had betrayed them. The Baobab stood silent; its twisted branches casting grotesque shadows over the scene, as if nature itself was mourning the lives lost that night.

But it wasn't enough for Thimmappa and Shivappa to simply kill the men who had destroyed their family. No, they wanted the whole village to know what had been done, to see the punishment they had delivered with their own hands. In a move that would haunt the village for years to come, the brothers mounted the bloodied heads of Mohan and Beerappa on the PatPati, strapping them to the front of the bike with a grim determination.

With the severed heads in place, they revved the engine, the sound of the sputtering bike cutting through the stillness of the night. As they rode through the mud roads, their faces set in stone, they made no attempt to hide their crime. Instead, they paraded through the village, the bloodied trophies bouncing with each bump in the road.

The villagers, roused from their sleep by the sound of the PatPati, came out of their homes, rubbing their eyes in confusion. But when they saw the gruesome sight before them, they gasped in horror. The sight of the severed heads, Mohan's eyes still wide in death, and Beerappa's lifeless expression, sent chills down their spines. Mothers pulled their children close, shielding them from the terrifying spectacle. Men stood in shocked silence, unable to comprehend the violence that had taken place.

The brothers said nothing as they rode through the village, their expressions unchanging. This wasn't a victory lap. This was a statement—a message to every landlord, every powerful man who thought he could exploit the weak without consequence. The people of the village had long been oppressed by men like Mohan and Beerappa, but tonight, they had seen something different. They had seen justice delivered by the hands of the oppressed themselves.

The PatPati's engine sputtered as the brothers disappeared into the darkness, leaving behind a trail of blood and fear. The village was left in stunned silence; the only sounds the faint rustling of the sugarcane fields and the distant howling of stray dogs.

By the time dawn broke over the dusty plains of Bijapur, word of the murders had spread far beyond the village. Some whispered that the brothers had fled to Mangalore, while others claimed they had been caught by the police. The village was on edge, fearful of what the landlords would do in retaliation.

A few days later, Rajappa received the news. Thimmappa and Shivappa had been arrested at Raichur station, trying to board a train. The police had taken them into custody, and now, they awaited their fate in the Bijapur jail.

The village may have momentarily reveled in the fall of the landlords' sons, but now, with the brothers in police custody, the tension grew palpable. Rajappa, still reeling from the tragedy that had befallen his sisters, knew they had no chance in the courts of Bijapur without proper legal representation. The villagers were too poor, too scared to help.

It was then, in the desperation of the moment that Rajappa had heard of a young lawyer, hailing from Bengaluru named Shastry, a man who had built a reputation for getting Bails with little or no fees and helping those who had no one else to turn to. Rajappa traveled over 650 kilometers to find Shastry, armed only with a plea for justice and the last of his family's meager savings.

As Rajappa stood in Shastry's office, recounting the horror of what had taken place in his village, Shastry knew that this case was more than just a legal battle—it was a fight for the very soul of a forgotten people, a people who had been denied justice for generations. Rajappa's family was in ruins. With no money and no hope, the case was being conducted by a legal aid lawyer who had filed a bail application at the Bijapur District Court. It had been rejected! Now, Rajappa stood before Shastry, desperate for help.

"Don't worry, Rajappa," Shastry said. "I'll handle this case. It won't be easy, but I'll do everything I can." Rajappa clasped Shastry's hand, his gratitude evident in his trembling voice. "Thank you, sir. You are our only hope."

Shastry's heart was pounding as Rajappa left. The weight of the responsibility hung heavy in the small office. This wasn't a simple bail application for a rowdy; this was a double-murder case with the prosecution relying on over 38 eyewitnesses. If he failed, the two brothers would likely spend their lives behind bars—or worse. But there was no turning back now.

Ramachandra Shastry leaned back in his worn-out swivel chair, contemplating the task ahead. Rajappa, the thin, weary man, had just handed over 25,000 rupees—his last savings, gathered by selling his only two oxen!

It wasn't nearly enough to cover the costs of traveling to Bijapur, filing a bail application at the High Court in

Kalburgi, and dealing with the complexities of trial in a double-murder case. Yet, the desperation in Rajappa's eyes, the raw need for justice, was enough for Shastry to accept the challenge.

This would be the first time Shastry would be moving a bail application under Section 439 of the Criminal Procedure Code before the Hon'ble High Court of Karnataka at Kalburgi. He had never appeared before the High Court in his young career, and the thought of it sent shivers down his spine. The case was complicated—two brothers, Shivappa and Thimmappa, accused of beheading two men and parading their severed heads through the village. The local police had acted swiftly, capturing the brothers and remanding them to judicial custody. The legal aid lawyer had tried and failed to get bail from the Bijapur District Court. Now, it was Shastry'sturn to try.

It was 11:30 p.m., and Shastry sat alone in his dimly lit office, the flickering tube light casting soft shadows across the room. The air was still, a sharp contrast to the buzz of activity that had filled the space just moments ago.

The last client had left, and now, for the first time that day, Shastry had a moment to breathe, to reflect. He lit a cigarette and the smell of tobacco filled his lungs, and for a fleeting second, it felt like time slowed down. The weight of the day settled over him, not with exhaustion, but with a quiet, satisfying triumph. He had earned Rs.75,000/- in a single day—a fortune compared to the humble beginnings of his practice. And more importantly, he had accepted a murder trial, a case that would take him to the Hon'ble High Court for the first time in his career as a lawyer enrolled in the BAR.

The gravity of it all made him pause. He smiled to himself, feeling at peace. The day had been long, but justice had been served, and hope had been restored in Rajappa's eyes. Shastry closed his eyes for a moment, his heart full of gratitude. Tonight, under the quiet glow of his modest office, he felt that maybe, just maybe, things were falling into place.

THE BIJAPUR TRAIL

Ramachandra Shastry stood at the bustling Majestic Bus Stand at 7:30 p.m., the next day, with the night air thick with the sounds of honking buses, shouting vendors, and the occasional distant roar of an engine. His eyes scanned the sea of red and white KSRTC buses until he spotted the one labeled "Bijapur." It was a government bus—old, rusted, and weathered by years of service, like a war-horse past its prime.

Shastry let out a soft chuckle and reached into his pocket, pulling out a slightly crumpled cigarette pack. He tapped it against his palm, extracting a single cigarette, andplaced it between his lips with a practiced elegance. Lighting it with the flick of a match, he took a slow, deliberate drag, the smoke curling around him like a mysterious fog. The orange glow of the cigarette tip illuminated his face as he exhaled a cloud of smoke, his mind already calculating the challenges that lay ahead in Bijapur.

This was his moment—the beginning of something bigger. As the chaotic bus stand continued its noisy existence around him, Shastry stood tall, smoking with the quiet confidence of a man who was ready to conquer whatever came next.

He took one final drag, flicked the cigarette to the ground, and crushed it underfoot with the heel of his shoe. The embers sizzled out as he shouldered his bag and stepped toward the bus, ready to face the long and uncertain journey ahead.

In an attempt to save money, Shastry decided to travel to Bijapur by KSRTC Red Bus, despite knowing the journey would be long and exhausting. The state bus station was bustling with travelers, many of whom seemed to be in as much of a hurry as Shastry felt. The rusting red-and-white government bus labeled "Bijapur" looked like it had seen better days, but it was the cheapest option available.

The moment he stepped inside the bus, the musty smell of years of unwashed upholstery hit him like a slap in the face. His optimism about the journey began to wane. The bus, which might have once been comfortable in its prime, now had seats that sagged in the middle like tired old men. It seemed every seat had seen better days—back when they weren't duct-taped together.

Shastry squeezed past a family of five who had somehow managed to occupy two seats, and finally reached seat number 37, which, to his dismay, was next to a large window covered with scratches and grime. He stuffed his bag into the overhead compartment and tried to sit down, only to realize that the seat cushion was practically nonexistent. It was as if the seat had been slowly devoured by time, leaving behind a thin, uncomfortable shell of its former self.

He shifted uncomfortably, trying to find a position that didn't feel like he was sitting on a pile of rocks. The bus's engine roared to life, and the entire vehicle vibrated as though it were a spaceship preparing for takeoff. With a loud screech, the bus lurched forward, and Shastry felt the jolt through his spine. He glanced out the window as they left the bus stand, watching as the glittering lights faded into the distance.

As the bus rattled its way out of Bengaluru, Shastry tried to prepare himself mentally for the case. He knew the legal theory well enough—*Mens Rea, Actus Reus, Reasonable Doubt*—but nothing could have prepared him for the challenges of traveling long distances with no resources. What he didn't know— and what he was about to find out the hard way—was that this overnight journey to Bijapur wasn't just long; it was excruciatingly long. The bus jerked and swayed on the pothole-riddled roads, and each bump threatened to dislodge his carefully constructed mental arguments.

The bus hurtled down the highway like a runaway bullock cart, bouncing over every pothole with reckless abandon. Each bump sent Shastry flying a few inches off his seat, his backside meeting the unforgiving frame of the chair again and again. By the time they had left the city limits, Shastry's tailbone had become intimately familiar with every spring poking out of the seat.

Around 11:00 p.m., Shastry's fellow passengers had started to settle in for the night. A symphony of snores erupted around him, making it impossible to sleep. The man next to him, a burly fellow with a penchant for chewing betel leaves, had already dozed off, his head lolling to the side and occasionally landing on Shastry's shoulder. Each time, Shastry nudged him back, only for the man to slump right back down like a puppet whose strings had been cut. Shastry clutched the armrests, his body lifting off the seat every few seconds as the bus hit another pothole. His teeth rattled with each jolt, and he silently cursed himself for not spending a little more money on a better bus.

The night wore on, and the temperature inside the bus began to drop. Shastry had made the fatal mistake of not bringing a blanket, thinking, how cold could it get? He was wrong. The wind howled through the cracks in the windows, and Shastry shivered in his thin cotton shirt, trying to curl into himself to conserve body heat. At one point, the bus made a sudden, jarring stop in the middle of nowhere. Shastry, startled awake, looked out the window. They had stopped at a roadside dhaba—a poorlylit shack that seemed to be held together by nothing but goodwill and a tin roof. The driver casually announced, "Tea break, ten minutes!" as the passengers stumbled out, groggy and irritated.

Shastry followed the crowd, grateful for the chance to stretch his legs. He ordered a cup of tea from the dhaba, which arrived in a glass that looked like it had seen a hundred such journeys. The tea was scalding hot, but it was strong enough to kick-start his senses. As he sipped, a stray dog wandered by and sat next to him, looking at him as if they were sharing the same existential crisis. Shastry's stomach growled, but he knew better than to trust the questionable food from these stalls. Instead, he stuck to his cigarette, letting the warmth of the tobacco fill his lungs.

After downing his tea, Shastry climbed back into the bus and braced himself for the next leg of the journey. The bus roared back to life, and what he didn't anticipate was the cold war that would soon erupt between thepassengers and the bus driver.

About two hours into the journey, the man sitting by the window next to Shastry decided that fresh air was a necessity. With a loud creak, he shoved the window open, letting a blast of icy wind rush in. The other passengers groaned, and a few shouted for him to close it, but the man was having none of it.

"*Close the window!*" someone shouted from the back.

"*It's freezing!*" another voice added.

But the man was unfazed. "Too stuffy inside!" he declared, his voice carrying over the rumble of the bus. "If you're cold, cover up!" I'll suffocate otherwise!" the man declared loudly, waving his hands for emphasis.

Shastry, who was now fully awake and freezing, tried to negotiate. "Sir, please... it's too cold. Maybe just open it halfway?"

The man shot him a look as though Shastry had suggested burning the bus down. The man scoffed. "Halfway won't help anyone. You'll thank me for this fresh air."

The window stayed open, and Shastry resigned himself to his fate, pulling his arms inside his shirt like a turtle retreating into its shell.

At some point, Shastry must have dozed off, because when he woke up, the sky was beginning to lighten. The bus was rumbling along a narrow road, bordered by open fields and distant hills. His back ached, his neck was stiff, and his clothes were wrinkled beyond recognition. But there was something oddly peaceful about the early morning countryside.

He checked his watch. 6:00 a.m. The journey wasn't over yet.

Just as he was starting to feel a glimmer of hope, the bus jerked violently, and Shastry was thrown against the window. A loud noise erupted from underneath the bus—an unsettling combination of screeching metal and grinding gears.

The driver pulled over to the side of the road, muttering curses under his breath as he climbed down to inspect the damage. Shastry, along with a few other curious passengers, got out of the bus to see what was going on.

Shastry, too tired to care, slumped back and lit another cigarette. He took a long, slow drag, watching the driver reappeared a few minutes later, wiping his hands on a rag. "Don't worry," he announced cheerfully. "Just a small issue with the axle. We'll be back on the road in no time!"

Shastry groaned and leaned back in his seat, silently praying for the bus to hold itself together for the remainder of the journey. Back on the bus, as the landscape paved way to the wide, arid expanses of northern Karnataka, Shastry found himself thinking about the case. The murder had taken place on a lonely mud road, far from the prying eyes of the village, but the brothers had ensured that everyone knew what had happened by parading the severed heads of Mohan and Beerappa on a *PatPati* (their battered Bajaj Splendor). It was the stuff of nightmares—a gruesome, macabre display of revenge that had sent shockwaves through the village.

The police had arrested Shivappa and Thimmappa within days, producing them before the magistrate and securing a swift remand to judicial custody. The case was now under the jurisdiction of the High Court in Kalburgi, far from Bijapur, where Shastry would have to file the bail application. It was an uphill battle from every angle—the legal aid lawyer had already failed to get bail, and the prosecution was armed with a list of 38 eyewitnesses. Shastry would need every ounce of skill and ingenuity to make this work.

Finally, at 11:30 a.m., after what felt like an eternity, the bus pulled into the Bijapur Bus Stand. Shastry stumbled off the bus, feeling as though he had aged ten years in one night. His clothes were disheveled, his eyes were bloodshot, and he was fairly certain he smelled like a combination of diesel fuel and stale tea. Shastry felt like a survivor emerging from a battlefield. His clothes were wrinkled beyond repair, his body ached from head to toe, and his head throbbed from the lack of sleep. But as he stepped off the bus and took in the sight of the ancient city, a sense of accomplishment washed over him. He had made it.

The streets of Bijapur were alive with the hum of daily activity. Vendors called out their wares, buses rumbled by, and the towering monuments of the Adil Shahi dynasty stood as a reminder of the city's storied past. Shastry lit one more cigarette, taking a long, thoughtful drag savoring it with tea, as he leaned against a pillar, surveying his surroundings.

The day was just beginning, and though the journey had been hellish, he was ready for what came next. The challenges of the murder trial, the High Court appearance, the heavy burden of justice—those would come soon enough. But for now, he was content to savor the moment—the quiet victory of simply arriving in Bijapur, with the weight of his mission still ahead. For now, his biggest challenge was finding a decent place to freshen up. He spotted a public dormitory nearby, the kind that offered basic amenities for travelers on a budget. It wasn't glamorous, but after the bus ride, Shastry wasn't in a position to be picky.

With little money to spare, he opted to stay in a public dormitory—a shared space where travelers could rest for a few rupees a night. It was far from luxurious. The walls were cracked, the shared bathroom questionable, and the bedding smelled faintly of sweat and stale air. But Shastry wasn't in a position to complain.

After a quick wash in the grimy communal bathroom, Shastry lay down on the narrow cot, exhaustion weighing on him. But sleep wouldn't come. His mind was racing, running through legal strategies and counterarguments, imagining how the prosecution would try to paint the brothers as cold-blooded killers.

He got up splashed cold water on his face, relishing the feeling of being somewhat human again. Once he was refreshed, his stomach reminded him that he hadn't eaten in hours. He wandered over to a nearby stall and ordered a plate of Mirchi Bajji with Susla—a simple yet spicy dish made of flattened rice, onions, and chilies.

As he took the first bite of the Green Mirchi bajji, the intense heat of the hit him like a punch to the face. His eyes watered, and he let out a small cough, much to the amusement of the vendor, who chuckled at the sight of the Bengaluru lawyer struggling with the local food.

But Shastry didn't mind. The Susla filled the gaping hole in his stomach, and the spicy kick brought a renewed energy to his body. By the time he finished, he was ready to take on whatever Bijapur had in store for him.

As he stood in the bustling streets, the morning suncasting long shadows on the ancient city, Shastry smiled to himself. The journey had been a comedy of errors, but it was behind him now. Ahead lay the biggest challenge of his legal career.

Shastry made his way to the Bijapur District Court to meet with the legal aid lawyer named Karneppa who had handled the case thus far. The man was polite but indifferent, clearly overwhelmed by his own workload. He handed Shastry the case file with a sigh, as if resigning himself to the inevitability of failure.

"It's a tough case," Karneppa said, shaking his head. "The prosecution has ironclad evidence, or so they think. And with 38 eyewitnesses to the parade, they're confident they'll secure a conviction order."

Shastry took the file, flipping through the pages. The evidence was damning—the post-mortem reports, the remand application, the spot mahazar documenting where the bodies had been found. But one key piece of evidence was missing: the Kattega, the locally forged sword used by Shivappa and Thimmappa to behead Mohan and Beerappa.

According to the legal aid lawyer, the brothers had disposed of the heads and the Kattega in the Bhima River, making it impossible for the police to recover the heads or the weapon as material objects. The prosecution had arranged for a substitute weapon to be produced in court, but it lacked the concrete link to the murders that the original sword would have provided.

Shastry saw a small window of opportunity. The absence of the murder weapon weakened the prosecution's case, though not by much. He would have to focus on the weaknesses in the autopsy and post mortem reports, the fact that the heads had never been recovered, and the possibility that some of the 38 eyewitnesses could be unreliable or coerced.

Next day, Shastry made his way to the Bijapur jail to meet with the accused—Shivappa and Thimmappa. The jail superintendent Arun Kumar, a gruff man with a perpetually tired expression, allowed him a brief interview. The brothers, shackled and weary, were led into a small, dimly lit room. Shivappa, the older of the two, did most of the talking. He recounted how, after the gruesome parade, they had fled the village and disposed of the heads and the sword in the Bhima River.

It was a night that was still, and the air carried a chill that clung to the skin. The full moon hung low over theDeccan plains, casting an eerie glow over the lonely mudroads of Bijapur. Shivappa and Thimmappa, their faces hardened by the weight of what they had just done, rode the battered PatPati—the Bajaj Splendor bike they had taken from their victims—through the fields, the decapitated heads of Mohan and Beerappa swaying from the front like grotesque trophies.

Their hearts raced, though not with fear or regret. What they felt now was a grim satisfaction, a dark justice for what had been done to their sisters. The mutilation of their family's honor had demanded more than just words—it had demanded blood.

They sped through the winding paths, the wind whipping against their faces, the path illuminated only by the pale moonlight. The plan was simple: dispose of the heads and the Kattega, the same sword that had severed them, into the "Bhima"—the famed River that wound its way through the ancient lands of Karnataka. The river had borne witness to centuries of life and death, its waters hiding more secrets than anyone could ever uncover. The Bhima was no ordinary river. For generations, it had been both a lifeline and a final resting place for those who sought to hide their sins. Legends swirled around the Bhima's quiet banks. Farmers and travelers spoke of bodies that had vanished in its depths, never to be found again.

Few months ago, there had been stories of a wealthy landlord who had thrown his rival into the Bhima, the man's hands bound with coarse rope, his mouth gagged with cloth so he couldn't scream. The landlord's crime was whispered about in the village for months, but without a body, there had been no justice. The river had swallowed him whole, silencing him forever.

Then there was the infamous tale of a woman from a nearby village who, tormented by her husband's infidelity, had drowned herself in the river's deep waters, taking with her their newborn child. The villagers had searched for days, but the river gave them nothing. Her spirit was said to haunt the waters on moonlit nights like this, her cries carried on the wind.

Shivappa wasn't superstitious, but the Bhima's reputation for swallowing people's secrets was the reason they had chosen it. The heads and the Kattega would be lost to its depths, leaving no trace for the authorities to find.

The bike came to a halt near the bank of the river, the sound of rushing water filling the silence around them. The brothers dismounted, their feet crunching against the soft sand. Before them, the Bhima River stretched wide, its waters black under the night sky, glistening like oil. The moon's reflection shimmered on the surface, giving the scene an almost otherworldly glow.

Thimmappa, the younger of the two, wiped the sweat from his brow, though the night was cool. His hands shook slightly—not from fear, but from the adrenaline that still coursed through his veins. The Kattega hung heavy at his side, its blade stained with the blood of the men they had killed. It was a crude weapon, forged in the village by a blacksmith who specialized in tools for animal sacrifice. But tonight, it had served a different purpose.

Without a word, Shivappa grabbed the two heads by their hair, his face expressionless. The weight of the heads felt strange in his hands, but he didn't let it show. The brothers approached the edge of the river, where the water lapped gently at the shore.

"We end it here," Shivappa said quietly, more to himself than to Thimmappa.

Thimmappa nodded, his eyes fixed on the river, its endless flow a reminder that life—and death—were constantly in motion. He handed Shivappa the Kattega, and for a moment, they both stood in silence, staring at the weapon that had changed their lives forever.

Shivappa stepped into the river, the cold water rising around his ankles. He waded in deeper, until the water reached his knees. Then, with a swift motion, he tossed the heads into the river, watching as they disappeared beneath the surface, swallowed by the black current.

"Gone," Thimmappa muttered, his voice barely audible.

The Kattega was next. Shivappa gripped the hilt, feeling the rough leather handle beneath his fingers. This sword had served its purpose, but it had no place in their future. With a final glance at the blade, he raised it high above his head and hurled it into the river. The sword hit the water with a splash, and then sank slowly into the depths, vanishing into the darkness.

For a moment, they both stood there, watching the ripples fade. The river was silent again, as though it had never been disturbed.

As they turned to leave, Thimmappa's gaze lingered on the water. The Bhima had done its job, just as they had done theirs. But what now? They had gotten their revenge, but the consequences were inevitable. The police would come looking for them, and soon enough, they would be found.

But for now, standing on the edge of the river, there was only a quiet satisfaction. The world felt different, as if the weight that had been pressing down on their hearts had been lifted. Their sisters had been avenged, and for that, the price was worth paying.

The Bhima River had taken their secret, just as it had taken countless others before. The brothers turned away from the water, their mission complete, and made their way back to the bike.

The night was still young, but somewhere in the distance, a dog howled, as if sensing the dark deeds that had unfolded by the riverbank. As Shivappa and Thimmappa rode away, the Bhima flowed on, eternal and unyielding, holding within its depths the unspeakable stories of those who had crossed its path.

"We knew the police would come for us," Shivappa said to Shastry, his voice calm but hollow. "So, we ran. But they caught us at Raichur railway station."

Thimmappa, younger and quieter, merely nodded in agreement. There was sadness in his eyes, a deep resignation to the fate that awaited them. Shastry asked a few more questions, gathering details about the incident, before having them sign the vakalathnama and the necessary legal papers.

MEMORIES DISTILLED

With the documents in hand—the order of rejection of the bail application, the chargesheet, the post-mortem report, and the other required materials—Shastry knew it was time to return to Bengaluru. The real work was just beginning.

By the time his work in Bijapur was done, Ramachandra Shastry felt both relieved and exhausted. The case had taken more out of him than he had anticipated. He had secured the necessary documents, spoken to the legal aid lawyer, and met with the accused brothers, Shivappa and Thimmappa. The gravity of the case still lingered in his mind, but tonight, he allowed himself a moment of indulgence.

Shastry had no intention of repeating the horrors of his last bus journey. The experience of being jostled around in the back of a rickety government bus had taught him a valuable lesson. So this time, he didn't experiment. He booked a ticket on a VRL sleeper bus, a far more luxurious option compared to the government-run red bus.

The bus was scheduled to depart at 10:00 p.m., and with more than a couple of hours to kill before boarding,

Shastry found himself wandering through the narrow streets of Bijapur. His thoughts turned to food—and drink.

As he strolled along the streets, Shastry spotted a small, unassuming liquor shop with a dusty signboard that read "Bijapur Wines". He grinned to himself, feeling the urge to unwind. Inside, he picked up a quarter of Old Monk, the familiar rum that had been a loyal companion through many sleepless nights during his college days. With the rum safely tucked under his arm, he headed to a nearby restaurant, a modest place where the aroma of freshly cooked biryani and spicy curries filled the air.

He took a seat at one of the corner tables, ordered a plate of mutton biryani, and sat back to enjoy his evening. The waiter brought him a glass of Thumbs Up, which Shastry poured over after adding a generous splash of Old Monk. The dark liquid fizzed and settled, and he stirred it with a spoon, watching the bubbles rise to the surface.

As he took his first sip, he felt the familiar warmth of the rum coursing through his veins. It was strong, with that unmistakable caramel sweetness, and it paired perfectly with the cold Thumbs Up. Leaning back in his chair, Shastry pulled out a cigarette, lit it, and took a deep drag. The smoke swirled around him, blending with the aromas of the restaurant, and he felt a wave of relaxation wash over him.

The evening breeze rustled through the open windows, and Shastry found himself lost in thought, contemplating the strategies he would use to win the case. His mind worked methodically, breaking down the chargesheet, analyzing the prosecution's reliance on eyewitnesses, and formulating a plan to exploit the gaps in their case. The missing weapon, the lack of forensic evidence—it was all swirling around in his head like the smoke from his cigarette.

Between sips of Old Monk and bites of mutton biryani, Shastry felt a rare sense of contentment. For the first time in days, he wasn't rushing from one task to the next. Here, in this small Bijapur restaurant, with the faint buzz of conversation and the clinking of plates around him, he could take a breath.

He extinguished his cigarette in the ashtray and poured himself another drink. The second and third peg went down smoother, the alcohol blending seamlessly with the Thumbs Up, loosening his muscles, and calming his thoughts. The heaviness of the day began to lift, replaced by a quiet confidence that he could handle what lay ahead.

Feeling satisfied and more than a little buzzed, Shastry checked his watch. It was almost time to board the bus. He paid the bill, pocketed his cigarettes, and made his way to the VRL bus stop, a short walk from the restaurant. The sleeper bus stood tall and pristine, a massive white and yellow behemoth compared to the humble red and white government buses he had endured on the way here.

This was luxury—a private sleeper berth awaited him, where he could actually lie down, stretch his legs, and get some sleep.

Shastry took one last puff of his cigarette, watching the smoke curl into the night sky before flicking the butt into the dustbin nearby. He boarded the bus, greeted by the cool blast of air-conditioning. The soft hum of the engine was already soothing as he climbed into his berth, which was surprisingly comfortable. It had a cushioned mattress, a proper pillow, and a clean blanket folded at the foot of the bed.

As the bus pulled out of the station, Shastry settled into his berth, reclining fully and adjusting the pillow beneath his head. He let out a long, contented sigh, feeling the rum settle warmly in his stomach. He wasn't sure if it was the Old Monk, the biryani, or the fact that he was on a far superior bus, but for the first time in days, he felt truly at ease.

As the bus swayed gently on the dark roads leading out of Bijapur, Shastry's thoughts drifted back to his law college days—those wild, rebellious years when everything changed for him, including his tastes and habits. Back then, he had been a different person. A young Brahmin boy, raised in a traditional vegetarian household where meat was considered taboo and Old Monk was something whispered about behind closed doors. His family followed their customs devoutly, and for most of his childhood, Shastry had been content with it. But Law College had a way of transforming people.

He still remembered his first encounter with non-vegetarian food. It had been a late night, after a particularly grueling day of lectures, case studies, and endless debates in the college canteen. His friends— Shekhar, Nagaraj, and Mohith—had convinced him to join them at a small, dingy restaurant near the college, the kind of place known for its spicy mutton curry and oily chicken kebabs. At first, Shastry had refused, sitting awkwardly with his plate of curd rice, watching his friends devour their plates of meat with gusto.

"Come on, Shastry," Shekar had teased, waving a piece of chicken kebab in front of him. "You're missing out on life. You've had enough of that curd rice for a lifetime. Just one bite!"

Shastry had hesitated, the Brahmin in him screaming NO, but the curiosity was overwhelming. It was more than peer pressure—something about the smell of the food, the camaraderie of the moment, made him want to give in. Mohith had shoved the plate closer, grinning mischievously, and in that moment, Shastry's resistance broke.

"Fine," he had said, almost defiantly, as if daring his upbringing to challenge him.

He had picked up a small piece of chicken and popped it into his mouth. The first bite was a revelation—the flavors of the spices, the richness of the meat, the way it melted in his mouth. It was unlike anything he had ever tasted. The guilt he expected never came; instead, he felt exhilarated, as if he had broken free of some invisible chain that had been holding him back.

From that day on, Shastry's taste buds expanded in ways he never thought possible. He began to explore the delights of biryanis, kebabs, and fish curries, learning to enjoy the fiery heat of the spices that clashed with the Brahmin restraint he had grown up with. What started as a hesitant step into unfamiliar territory soon became a part of who he was.

The transition from vegetarian to non-vegetarian was only half the story. Around the same time, Shastry had also developed a love for Old Monk rum, the legendary Indian Rum that was a rite of passage for many law students. It had started innocently enough, during one of those endless nights of studying for exams. His friends, always, had brought a bottle of Old Monk to their study session, insisting that a little drink would help them "focus."

"Shastry, you need to loosen up, man!" Mohith had said, pouring a glass of rum mixed with Coke. "How are you going to argue in court if you can't even handle a drink?"

At first, Shastry had laughed them off, determined to stick to his tea. But as the hours dragged on and the pressure of studying mounted, he found himself staring at the amber liquid, its dark, rich color calling to him.

"Just one glass," he had told himself, as he took the glass from Shekhar.

The first sip had been tentative, the taste unfamiliar yet surprisingly pleasant. It was strong, yes, but there was something comforting about the way the warmth of the rum spread through his chest. He had taken another sip, and then another, feeling the weight of the night lift with each swallow.

Old Monk soon became his drink of choice during their late-night study sessions and even more so during their celebrations after exams or moot court victories. Paired with spicy non-vegetarian food, it created a perfect storm of flavors that Shastry began to crave. He had started with small sips, but by the time he was in his final year, Shastry had developed a taste for both Old Monk and the chicken kebabs that often accompanied it.

He still remembered the nights spent on the terrace of their friend Nagaraj's house, under the open sky, the sounds of the city far below. The four of them—Shastry, Nagaraj, Mohith, and Shekhar—would sit in a circle, bottles of Old Monk and plates of biryani between them, smoking cigarettes and debating everything from law to life. It was during these nights that Shastry truly learned the art of argument, the careful balance between passion and logic. The rum would loosen their tongues, but it never clouded their sharp minds.

For Shastry, those nights were formative, not just for his love of Old Monk and non-veg food, but for the camaraderie and the sense of freedom it brought. It was where he found his voice, his conviction to push against boundaries—both personal and professional.

As Shastry lay in the sleeper berth of the VRL bus, the memories of those Law College days came rushing back. He could almost taste the chicken kebab again, smell the smoke from the cigarettes they used to light after their meals, and feel the warmth of Old Monk spreading through his veins. Those had been the nights where everything seemed possible, where they had all believed that they would conquer the world one case at a time.

He took a deep breath, the faint scent of his recent cigarette still lingering on his clothes, and smiled to himself. Despite being raised in a strict Brahmin household, he had embraced a new way of life, a blend of the old and the new. His love for the law, his newfound taste for non-vegetarian food, and his appreciation for a strong drink like Old Monk—it was all part of who he had become.

Shastry shifted in his berth, pulling the blanket closer around him. The bus hummed along the highway, its gentle rocking lulling him into a peaceful state. Tonight, he wasn't worried about the case, or the complexities of the legal arguments that lay ahead. Tonight, he was simply content, his mind wandering back to the days when everything had started to change.

And as he drifted into sleep, he couldn't help but feel grateful—for the friends who had pushed him to try something new, for the nights of rum-fueled debates, and for the journey that had led him here, ready to take on the biggest challenge of his career.

THE ART OF INQUIRY

It had been ten days since Ramachandra Shastry returned from Bijapur, and his mind was consumed by the murder case. The stakes were high—his first real shot at arguing before the High Court in Kalburgi, for bail on behalf of two brothers accused of a gruesome double murder. Shastry knew that if he didn't prepare thoroughly, he'd have no chance of securing bail for his clients, Shivappa and Thimmappa.

Every day since returning, Shastry made his way to the High Court library in Bengaluru. It had become his second home and probably the best place in the whole of universe for Shastry, where he spent hours pouring over criminal law books, old case files, and legal commentaries.

The librarian, a grumpy old man with spectacles perched precariously on the tip of his nose, hadquickly learned to dread Shastry's daily visits.

"Sir, that ladder," Shastry called out, pointing towards the tall, movable ladder used to access the higher shelves of the library. "I need it again, please."

The librarian, barely looking up from his newspaper, grumbled under his breath. "You're going to break your neck one of these days."

"I'll risk it. Today, I need the sections on conspiracy and murder. Somewhere near the top, I believe," Shastry replied with a grin, already making his way toward the ladder. He climbed with the enthusiasm of a child in a candy shop, the ladder creaking as he reached for an old volume on homicide.

Shastry often felt like a detective on the hunt for the perfect clue. He would fast-read through pages, sometimes standing halfway up the ladder, other times precariously balancing on the top rung as he scribbled down notes in his leather-bound notebook. His speed reading was legendary among the other students, but his ability to extract key legal principles had to be honed.

One day, as he was perched high up on the ladder, furiously flipping through a Supreme Court ruling on bail in homicide cases, the ladder wobbled. The librarian, looking up from his desk, raised an eyebrow.

"You're either going to crack open a case or crack open your skull!" he shouted, shaking his head.

"Both," Shastry quipped, barely paying attention. "But hopefully the case first."

Late into the tenth day, with his notebook filled with legal precedents and notes from old rulings, Shastry returned to his office. He sat at his desk, staring at the blank page in front of him, his fingers drumming lightly on the table. Drafting the bail application wasn't going to be easy, but the case depended on it. He had to make it bulletproof, exploiting every loophole and weakness in the prosecution's case.

He lit a cigarette, took a slow drag, and exhaled, letting the smoke curl around his head as he started drafting the application. The words came slowly at first, but then flowed with clarity and purpose. Each ground for bail had to be meticulously crafted, each argument sharpened to perfection. He laid down the grounds:

NO CRIMINAL ANTECEDENTS: This was the foundation— Shivappa and Thimmappa had no prior criminal history. They weren't hardened criminals, just two brothers from a small village caught in a tragic situation.

THE RECOVERED WEAPON'S IMPOSSIBILITY: "Recovered weapon at no stretch of imagination could have taken off two human heads."

The Kattega, the alleged murder weapon, had been thrown into the Bhima River and was never recovered. The prosecution had presented a substitute weapon, but Shastry would argue that it was impossible for such a weapon to have caused the beheadings.

NO EYEWITNESS TO THE ACTUAL CRIME:

"No eyewitnesses saw the severing of the heads." While many had seen the grisly parade, no one had witnessed the moment of the murders. This was a crucial gap in the prosecution's case.

THE DISTRICT COURT'S FLAWED RULING:

The rejection of bail by the District Court had been emotional, based on the horror of the crime rather than the legal merits. Shastry intended to point that out. Bail is the Rule, Jail is the Exception: Shastry wrote this line with emphasis, drawing from landmark Supreme Court rulings:

"Bail is the rule, and jail is the exception. This principle has been upheld by the Hon'ble Supreme Court in various rulings and must apply to the present case as well."

He had read countless judgments where the Supreme Court had reaffirmed this principle. In cases of serious offenses, even when the evidence appeared damning, bail had been granted when the prosecution had failed to establish a solid prima facie case.

DEPRIVATION AND SOCIAL BACKGROUND:

This was a final appeal to the court's compassion. Shivappa and Thimmappa were not cold-blooded killers—they were villagers who had snapped under the weight of unbearabletragedy.

Satisfied with the structure, Shastry leaned back and took another drag of his cigarette, exhaling slowly as he admired his work. But the real challenge was still ahead—

he had to travel to Kalburgi, file the case, and argue it before the High Court.

Hon'ble High Court of Karnataka at Kalburgi

Shastry boarded a train from Bengaluru to Kalburgi the following evening, his nerves on edge. As the train rattled along the tracks, he sat by the window, the distant glow of passing villages flickered by like forgotten memories, and he couldn't help but think of what awaited him.

Kalburgi, the city of domes, was once a seat of power for the Bahmani Sultanate, a kingdom that dominated the Deccan region in the 14th century. Its name, derived from the word Kaluburgi—meaning stone fort—was a testament to the city's historical importance as a military stronghold. As the train sped through the countryside, Shastry imagined the ancient walls of the Gulbarga Fort, towering above the city, their stones whispering stories of battles, royal courts, and political intrigue.

Shastry had read about the fort, a magnificent relic of medieval architecture, with its Jama Masjid, modeled after the great mosque of Córdoba in Spain. The mosque, with its arches and large domes, stood within the fort, almost as if guarding the city's ancient spirit. As a history enthusiast, Shastry was fascinated by how Kalburgi had once been a vibrant hub of trade, culture, and military power under the Bahmani dynasty, before the capital moved to Bidar.

He pictured the streets of Kalburgi, bustling with traders from all corners of the region—spices, silk, and jewels passing through the hands of merchants, while poets and scholars debated in the royal courts, adding to the city's rich cultural tapestry. The city had also played a significant role in the spread of Sufism in the Deccan region, becoming a center for mystics and Sufi saints. The revered Hazrat Khwaja Banda Nawaz, whose tomb still attracts pilgrims, was a figure deeply embedded in Kalburgi's spiritual fabric.

Kalburgi was foreign to him—a distant, unfamiliar city with a reputation for being slow and bureaucratic. Shastry had never filed a case in the High Court, and he had no contacts there. It would be an uphill battle.

As dawn began to break, Shastry felt the train slow as it approached Kalburgi station. The orange hue of the morning sun bathed the land, casting long shadows over the open fields. The train rolled into the station with a screech, and Shastry stepped onto the platform, stretching his legs after the long night. Kalburgi greeted him with the scent of fresh earth and the distinct aroma of karid rotti being fried at a nearby stall.

The station, though bustling, carried a certain warmth. The vendors, their voices rising above the hum of the crowd, offered steaming plates of mirchi bhajji and karid rotti—the kind of food that sticks to your bones and reminds you of home. Shastry couldn't resist the temptation. He ordered a plate of bhajji and a hot cup of Kahwa, the local saffron-infused tea. The first bite of the bhajji, crispy on the outside and soft on the inside, paired with the spicy tang of the green chili, sent a warmth through him, in the cool morning air.

Shastry arrived at Kalburgi Railway Station and his arrival at the lodge was anything but grand. The lodge, if you could even call it that, stood precariously between a rundown tea stall and a narrow alleyway that seemed to lead nowhere. As he walked in, his hopes of finding a decent place to stay immediately crumbled. The lobby was dimly lit by a single flickering bulb, and the receptionist, an old man who looked like he'd been part of the lodge since its foundation, greeted him with a yawn.

"Room number 4. Top floor," the man mumbled, handing Shastry a rusty key without even looking up from his newspaper.

Shastry ascended the creaking staircase, which seemed to moan under the weight of each step, as if protesting his decision to stay here. The hallway on the top floor was narrow and smelled faintly of stale curry and musty carpets. By the time he reached room number 4, he felt like he'd been transported into a parallel universe—one where basic hygiene and hospitality were long-forgotten concepts.

The room itself was... well, functional. A single bed with a mattress so thin that it seemed to mock the idea of comfort, a ceiling fan that spun lazily as if deciding whether to actually circulate any air, and a window that offered a glorious view of the back alley's overflowing garbage bins. But the pièce de résistance was the bathroom—a tiny space with a bucket that had seen better days, and a showerhead that looked more like a relic from an archaeological dig.

Shastry sighed. This was going to be home for the next few days.

Determined to make the best of it, he decided to freshen up. He filled the bucket with cold water, splashing his face with enthusiasm. The water, however, was so cold that it felt like someone had dumped ice sourced straight from the Morturyǃ Shastry gasped, his mind suddenly sharp, as if he'd just received an electric jolt. He looked in the cracked mirror above the sink, water dripping from his face. "This is how legends are made," he muttered to himself, trying to laugh it off.

That night, as Shastry lay on the bed, staring at the ceiling, the fan made a noise that was somewhere between a groan and a whine. Every time he thought it might pick up speed, it slowed back down, leaving him in a constant state of sweaty limbo. He turned to his side, attempting to find a position that didn't feel like lying on a pile of cardboard, but it was no use. The bed seemed determined to add insult to injury.

Suddenly, a mosquito buzzed by his ear—a tiny but persistent enemy. Shastry clapped his hands in the air, trying to swat it away, only to knock over the glass of water on the nightstand. The water spilled all over his phone and the important case papers he had brought with him. "Fantastic," Shastry sighed, as he leapt out of bed to save his documents from the mini-flood.

He sat back on the bed, exhausted but too hot and uncomfortable to sleep. He pulled out a cigarette, lit it, and leaned back, the dim glow of the streetlight casting a shadow on his tired face. Smoke curled up toward the ceiling, blending with the lazy fan that still refused to do its job.

"Kalburgi hospitality at its finest," he thought wryly, puffing out a stream of smoke. But deep down, even in this tiny, uncomfortable room, Shastry knew this was part of the adventure. The case was important, and for now, he'd have to endure the lodge's less-than-stellar conditions. After all, the stories worth telling never start with comfort.

Next day Shastry made his way to the High Court counter to file his bail application. He handed the clerk his application with a sense of accomplishment. But his optimism quickly faded as the clerk gave him a bored look.

"It'll take three days to process and scrutinize your application for office objections!" the clerk said without even looking at the application.

"Three days?" Shastry exclaimed. "Why so long?"

The clerk shrugged, completely indifferent to Shastry's urgency. "That's the way it works here. You can check back on the third day."

Shastry felt his temper rising, but he knew better than to argue. He took a deep breath and stepped outside, lighting a cigarette to calm his nerves. The process was going to be excruciatingly slow, and there was nothing he could do about it.

For the next three days, Shastry lived like a nomad in Kalburgi, staying in a rundown lodge near the city center, eating at small roadside stalls, and spending his evenings smoking on the lodge balcony, contemplating the case. He barely had enough money to cover his stay for the numerous appearances he would have to be at Bijapur also, but he managed to scrape by, determined not to leave until the case was listed.

Filing the case had been the easy part. Getting it listed for a hearing was another ordeal altogether. Each day, he stood in long lines at the court, waiting for his turn to speak with clerks and judges' assistants, trying to grease the wheels of bureaucracy. The system was slow and bloated, but Shastry had no choice but to persist. Shastry spent hours waiting in lines, trying to get the right signatures, the correct stamps, the necessary approvals. Each step of the process felt like an uphill battle. The clerks were slow, some indifferent, others simply too buried in paperwork to care.

For three days, Shastry moved from counter to counter, his patience thinning with every passing hour. He smoked cigarette after cigarette outside the court, the smoke blending with the dust of the city streets. At times, he questioned whether he was in over his head—whether this case was more than he could handle. But then he remembered Rajappa, the man who had come to him in desperation, and Shivappa and Thimmappa, who were languishing in jail, waiting for their lives to be decided.

On the fourth day, after what felt like an eternity, the case was finally listed. As Shastry sat down to catch his breath, he looked around the city once more. The grand domes of Kalburgi's mosques, the chatter of the vendors, the scent of spices wafting through the air—it all felt surreal. He had complied with all the office objections and the bail application was finally ready to be listed for hearing. Shastry felt a surge of relief as he saw the date confirmed on the list.

Kalburgi had tested him, pushed him to his limits, but it had also given him the resolve to fight. Shastry lit one last cigarette before the day's end, watching the smoke curl into the evening sky. The city had a way of pulling you in, forcing you to confront yourself, and Shastry felt that by walking its streets, he had become a little stronger, a little more resilient.

As the sun began to set over Kalburgi, Shastry knew that the real battle would begin tomorrow, in the High Court. But for now, he allowed himself to savor the moment, to admire the city that had so effortlessly blended history, culture, and survival into something uniquely its own.

Next day Shastry headed towards the High Court. The towering walls of the Hon'ble High Court of Karnataka at Kalburgi seemed to close in on Shastry as he stepped into the grand courtroom. It was the first time he would argue a case before the High Court, and the weight of the moment clung to him like the heavy robes he wore. His heart pounded against his chest, each thud amplifying the realization that this was no ordinary courtroom, and this was no ordinary case. His clients, Shivappa and Thimmappa, accused of the double murder of Mohan and Beerappa, had placed their faith in him. The stakes couldn't have been higher.

The courtroom was massive, filled with rows of junior and senior advocates, their eyes darting between case files and each other. As Shastry made his way to the front, he could feel the tension mounting. Shastry sat at the far endof the packed Hon'ble High Court of Karnataka at Kalburgi, his eyes fixed on the long list of cases. His case, No. 24 on List No. 1, was still a few numbers away, but every passing moment only added to his anxiety. The courtroom was large, its air-conditioning humming softly, but despite the cool breeze, Shastry could feel the sweat trickling down his back. His palms were slick, and he had already wiped them on his robe several times. Sitting at the bench was Justice Shivaprasad Sharma, a man known for his integrity, intellect, and piercing questions.

Shastry had heard of him many times—stories of how Justice Sharma dissected arguments with cold precision, asking questions that cut through even the most prepared counsel like arrows dipped in poison. There was no room for error in this courtroom, especially not with Justice Sharma presiding. The man was not known for outbursts or anger, but for the precision of his questions. He had a reputation for dissecting arguments with the same meticulousness as a surgeon with a scalpel. Justice Sharma's questions were never loud, but they were devastating—each one calculated, probing the weak spots in counsel's submissions like a hot knife cutting butter.

The courtroom was full that morning, with juniors and senior advocates alike filling the benches. A soft murmur of voices filled the room as the senior members of the BAR whispered to each other, waiting for their turns. Shastry sat rigidly, his stomach twisted into knots. The sweat on his forehead refused to stop despite the air-conditioned air that swirled around him.

"Shivappa and Anr v. State of Karnataka, listed as Item 24," the court clerk finally called.

Shastry felt his heart lurch. He swallowed hard, adjusted his gown, and rose to his feet. It was time. He gathered his case file, took a deep breath, and walked toward the bar, every step feeling heavier than the last.

Justice Sharma, seated at the bench, gazed at him impassively. His sharp features and stern eyes gave nothing away, but Shastry could feel the intensity of the judge's presence. The soft rustling of papers in the courtroom quieted down as everyone turned their attention to the case.

Shastry stood, feeling the weight of every eye in the courtroom on him. His mouth was dry, and his legs felt unsteady as he approached the bench. He had meticulously prepared for this moment, spending sleepless nights in his tiny lodge room, reading and rereading case laws, memorizing precedents, and drafting and redrafting his arguments. But now, standing before the court, all those preparations seemed a distant memory, replaced by a growing sense of urgency.

Shastry cleared his throat and began. "May it please Your Lordship," he said his voice more confident than he felt. "I appear on behalf of the Petitioners, Shivappa and Thimmappa, who have been accused of a double murder under Section 302 of the IPC. I am here seeking bail under Section 439 of the Cr.PC."

Justice Sharma gave a slight nod, his gaze never leaving Shastry. "Proceed, Mr. Shastry. We are listening."

"My Lords, the prosecution's case against my clients is built on fragile ground. The Petitioners are accused of an atrocious act—a double murder. But we cannot let the gruesome nature of the crime cloud the principles of justice. There is no prima facie evidence directly linking my clients to the commission of the murder."

Justice Sharma leaned forward slightly, his eyebrows raised. "Mr. Shastry, are you suggesting that the parade of the severed heads, witnessed by multiple people, is not enough to establish a link to the crime?"

Shastry took a deep breath and launched into his arguments, starting with the lack of prima facie evidence. "The prosecution, in its zeal to present a compelling narrative, has introduced a weapon into evidence—the so-called Kattega, a crude village sword. They assert that this weapon was used by my clients to sever the heads of Mohan and Beerappa. But, My Lords, I stand here today to vehemently submit that the weapon in question could not, under any stretch of imagination, cause such an injury."

A murmur ran through the courtroom, but Justice Sharma raised a hand, and silence returned almost instantly. His sharp gaze never wavered from Shastry.

"Proceed, Mr. Shastry," the judge said calmly, his voice inviting Shastry to continue but with an undertone that promised tough questions ahead.

Shastry nodded, feeling the surge of adrenaline course through him. This was his moment. "My Lords, the weapon being produced by the prosecution—a Kattega, commonly used in villages for agricultural purposes or for animal sacrifices—is simply inadequate to perform such a precise beheading. The autopsy report of both victims reveals that the severing of the heads was done in one clean stroke—a single, precise cut. Yet, the weapon the prosecution places before this Court is a dull, heavy blade that could hardly be used to decapitate a human, let alone achieve such precision."

Shastry reached into his brief, pulling out the autopsy report and waving it lightly for emphasis. "This report, My Lords, clearly states that the injury was caused by a sharp-edged weapon, one with a high degree of precision and sharpness, not the blunt, rusty Kattega currently being presented."

Justice Sharma's eyebrows raised slightly, his pen tapping gently against the desk. "Are you suggesting, Mr. Shastry, that the prosecution is presenting the wrong weapon? Or are you implying that no weapon of this kind could have been used at all?"

Shastry anticipated this question and leaned in, his voice growing more fervent. "My Lords, what I am submitting is two-fold: first, that the weapon before us is not the weapon which is allegedly used in the crime. It lacks the sharpness, precision, and weight distribution needed to cause the type of clean cut found in the autopsy. Second, I suggest that the prosecution's case is built on speculation, not evidence. They have presented a weapon merely for the sake of presentation, to satisfy the emotional outrage of the public, not to establish facts."

Justice Sharma's pen stopped mid-tap. The room held its collective breath.

"The prosecution," Shastry continued, "has failed to establish any scientific connection between the weapon and the injuries. No forensic examination was conducted to verify if this weapon could, in fact, cause the clean beheadings. I have reviewed the statements—there is no mention of any blood trace or human tissue on the weapon. It was conveniently 'found' and introduced without any link to the actual crime."

Shastry paused for effect, allowing the weight of his words to sink in. He could feel the courtroom buzzing quietly, as if everyone present could sense the cracks in the prosecution's case.

Justice Sharma looked down at the weapon list, flipping through a few pages. "Mr. Shastry, you are aware, are you not, that intent and execution of a crime are just as significant as the tools used to commit it? If your clients intended to kill and succeeded, does the exact weapon matter as much as the result of their actions?"

Shastry's heart raced. The judge had asked a question that pierced to the heart of the argument. But Shastry was ready. He leaned forward slightly, his voice dropping to a more impassioned tone, as though addressing the judge directly across from him in an intimate conversation.

"My Lords, with the highest respect, I submit that the weapon matters greatly. The prosecution's entire case is built on the assertion that my clients used this specific Kattega to commit these beheadings. If the weapon they present cannot have caused the injuries, then their theory of the crime collapses."

He lifted the autopsy report higher. "We cannot decide based on public perception, My Lord. We cannot imprison my clients based on assumptions. The law demands facts. And the fact is, this weapon cannot be the one that caused these fatal injuries."

Justice Sharma's eyes flicked back to the prosecution's side of the courtroom. The silence from their table was deafening. The judge leaned back slightly, his fingers steepled as he considered Shastry's point.

Justice Sharma raised his eyebrow slightly, his pen tapping lightly on the desk. "Mr. Shastry, are you suggesting that the lack of weapon weakens the case to such an extent that bail should be granted?"

Shastry felt the weight of the question press down on him. "Yes, My Lords. The absence of these material objects creates a significant gap in the prosecution's case. Furthermore, none of the eyewitnesses can testify to having seen the actual murder. They only have claimed to have witnessed the gruesome parade of the heads afterward."

Justice Sharma's gaze sharpened. "You are aware, Mr. Shastry, that mere mens rea—the intent to kill—can be sufficient to deny bail in heinous crimes, even if the exact weapon is not recovered. The parade of heads alone suggests a level of brutality that the court cannot ignore."

Shastry's mind raced. He had anticipated this question, but it still stung. He gathered his thoughts, his voice steady. "My Lords, I am not disregarding the gravity of the crime. However, the legal principle is clear. Without strong, irrefutable evidence directly linking my clients to the act of murder; keeping them in jail amounts to punishing them before trial. We must weigh the need for justice against the rights of the accused."

Justice Sharma remained silent for a moment, his eyes piercing into Shastry's. The room was so quiet that Shastry could hear the soft buzz of the air conditioning. Every pair of eyes in the courtroom was on him, waiting for the judge's response.

Shastry could feel his pulse quicken. The judge was closing in. "My Lords, with utmost respect, I submit that bail is the rule, and jail is the exception, as laid down by the Hon'ble Supreme Court in State of Rajasthan v. Balchand, 1977 AIR 2447 and followed in several precedents. The Petitioners hail from a deprived community. They are the sole breadwinners of their family, and prolonged incarceration without trial would be an excessive punishment before guilt is established."

As Shastry sat down, still processing, he felt a sudden shift in the atmosphere of the courtroom. The faint shuffle of papers, the murmurs of junior lawyers, and the soft creaking of wooden benches seemed to fade into the background. All attention was now focused on the senior public prosecutor, Mr. Rajshekhar Idgundi, who rose with the deliberate confidence of a man who had been through countless high-profile cases.

Rajshekhar Idgundi, an imposing figure in his mid-fifties with silver streaks in his well-groomed hair, had built a formidable reputation in the legal fraternity. He was a senior member of the BAR, known for his incisive arguments, and someone who had mastered the art of delivering a verbal blow that left the opposing counsel reeling. His presence in court was always commanding, and today was no different. Shastry watched him with a sense of impending dread.

Idgundi adjusted his black gown, his fingers brushing lightly over the podium as he prepared to speak. There was no rush, no anxiety in his movements. He knew his arguments were solid, and now it was time to deliver the final blow that would crush Shastry's defense.

"May it please Your Lordship," Idgundi began, his voice measured, deep, and brimming with authority. He didn't need theatrics; his voice alone was enough to silence the room.

"The defense has skillfully attempted to paint this case as one that lacks sufficient material evidence—particularly with respect to the weapon. But, My Lords, I stand here to firmly submit that the contentions taken by the Petitioners do not diminish the gravity of this crime, nor does it undermine the evidence that points to the accused's guilt."

Justice Sharma's gaze settled on Idgundi, his sharp eyes attentive. It was clear that the judge had been impressed by Shastry's argument, but Idgundi was about to dismantle it piece by piece.

Idgundi took a step forward, locking his gaze onto the judge. "My Lords, let us not be swayed by the technicality of evidence. The argument about the weapon's inability to cause such beheadings is not a sufficient ground for granting bail. In fact, the law does not require the weapon to be present or even recovered in cases where the crime is heinous and the intent is clear. The prosecution's case rests not on the absence of material objects but on the overwhelming evidence of intent and the terror unleashed by the accused."

He paused, allowing his words to settle over the courtroom, before continuing with increased intensity. "The accused, Shivappa and Thimmappa, did not simply kill these men. They paraded their heads in a public act of brutality, intending to send a message—a message of fear, terror, and domination. This act was premeditated, cold-blooded, and designed to strike fear into the hearts of an entire village."

Justice Sharma remained silent, his eyes narrowing as Idgundi continued, delivering his arguments with the precision of a seasoned warrior. Shastry watched in silent awe, knowing this was the moment when Idgundi would deliver the sucker punch.

"Furthermore, Your Lordship, the defense has argued that the eyewitnesses did not see the actual beheading. But do we need to? What the village witnessed was more than enough to prove the depravity of these acts. Thirty-eight people, My Lords, saw the accused parading through the streets, holding those heads as trophies. This was not an act of passion. This was an act of terror. The intent was to inflict psychological harm on an entire community, not just the victims."

The courtroom seemed to shrink under the weight of Idgundi's words. He glanced briefly at Shastry, the hint of a smile playing at the corners of his mouth. He knew his argument was landing.

Idgundi turned back to the judge. "My Lords, I would like to submit that the Hon'ble Supreme Court in a plethora of cases held that in cases of gruesome murder, especially where the intent to terrorize and inflict psychological damage is clear, the courts must exercise extreme caution in granting bail. The Apex Court emphasized that public confidence in the justice system must be maintained in such cases."

He flipped through his papers with practiced ease. "Moreover, the Hon'ble Supreme Court reiterated that in crimes of this nature, where public order and peace are disturbed, the Court must weigh the interests of society over the personal liberty of the accused. In the case at hand, releasing the accused on bail would not only be a disservice to the victims and their families but would shake the very foundation of law and order in the community."

Justice Sharma's face remained impassive, but Shastry could sense that Idgundi's words were sinking in. The public prosecutor had masterfully shifted the focus from the technical aspects of the case to the emotional and societal impact of the crime. This was the sucker punch that Shastry had feared—a blow that struck at the heart of the argument and cast the crime in a light that transcended mere legalities.

Idgundi's voice took on a tone of finality, the weight of his years of experience bearing down on the courtroom. "My Lords, this is not a case where we are merely dealing with two individuals accused of murder. This is a case where the accused sought to inflict terror on an entire community. They used the severed heads as a symbol of dominance, instilling fear that has lingered long after the crime was committed. They did not just kill two men—they tried to destroy the spirit of a village."

He stepped back from the podium slightly, his eyes unwavering as he delivered the final blow. "The defense has tried to focus on technical details, on missing evidence, but I urge this Court to see the larger picture. This is not a case where bail should be granted. The accused, by their actions, have forfeited their right to liberty. I request Your Lordship to dismiss the bail application and send a clear message that such acts of terror and brutality will not be tolerated."

The courtroom was silent, everyone hanging on the edge of Idgundi's final words. Justice Sharma remained still, his gaze flickering between the prosecution and the defense, deep in thought. Shastry felt the weight of the prosecutor's words pressing down on him. He knew Idgundi had struck at the core of the case, casting it in a moral and societal frame that was hard to challenge.

After what felt like an eternity, Justice Sharma finally spoke, his voice calm but decisive. "Mr. Idgundi, your arguments are well-constructed and raise important concerns.

The Court acknowledges the brutal nature of thecrime and the psychological harm inflicted on the village.It is clear that the actions of the accused go beyond meremurder—they sought to instill fear and terror. The law must protect society from such heinous acts."

Sharma glanced at Shastry, his voice softening just slightly. "Mr. Shastry, your arguments have been passionate and well-presented, and I commend your effort. However, the mens rea and actus reus are both evident in this case. The law cannot overlook the severity of the crime. Public interest and justice demand caution." Shastry's heart sank. He had seen it coming but had hoped for a miracle.

"While this Court appreciates your effort, the Petitioners' actions have created a climate of fear and horror in the village. Public confidence in the justice system must be upheld. The bail application is dismissed."

Shastry felt a knot tighten in his stomach. It was over. He had fought hard, but the case was too grim, too filled with public outrage for the Court to grant bail. The sound of the gavel echoed in his ears, final and unyielding.

As Shastry gathered his papers, preparing to leave, Justice Sharma spoke again, his tone unexpectedly warm. "Mr. Shastry, before you leave, let me say this: you argued your case with commendable passion and integrity. Your arguments were clear, well-structured, and showed an understanding of the complexities involved. It is not often that I see young advocates argue with such conviction."

Shastry, surprised, looked up. Justice Sharma continued, "Though the facts of this case did not allow for a favorable outcome, I foresee a bright future for you in the legal profession. Keep up the hard work, and one day, your efforts will yield success. You are on the right path."

The praise, coming from a man of Justice Sharma's stature, felt like a small victory. Shastry offered a grateful nod, his spirits lifted, even if just a little.

"Thank you, My Lords," Shastry said, his voice sincere.

With that, Shastry turned and walked out of the courtroom, the weight of the day's proceedings still heavy on his shoulders, but with a newfound sense of purpose ignited within him. The road ahead was long, but the seeds of growth had been planted. The gavel came down with a soft thud, final and unyielding. "The bail application is dismissed."

Shastry exhaled slowly, feeling the crushing weight of the decision, but knowing deep down that Idgundi's argument had been flawless—a true sucker punch that left no room for retreat.

As he packed up his papers, Shastry glanced over at Idgundi, who gave him a brief, respectful nod before turning back to his seat. It was the acknowledgment of a seasoned veteran to a young lawyer, and though Shastry had lost the battle, he knew he had earned the respect of one of the best in the business.

The case was over, but the lessons would last a lifetime. The setting sun cast an orange glow over the ancient city of Kalburgi as Shastry stood on the narrow balcony of his lodge, staring out at the fading light with a cigarette lit in his hand. The city, which had felt so foreign and full of possibility when he first arrived, now seemed cold and distant. His chest tightened with the weight of disappointment, and the soft hum of the street below only deepened the silence within him. His bail application had been rejected.

It wasn't just the verdict—it was the culmination of days of sleepless nights, countless hours spent in preparation, and endless frustrations in an unfamiliar city that had tested his patience, his skills, and his spirit. He had journeyed from Bengaluru with hope, with belief that his passion, his determination, and his sense of justice would be enough. But as he sat there, packing his backpack in the dim light of the room, the reality of his failure settled over him like a cold, damp blanket.

He had rented a tiny room in an inconvenient lodge with a bed that creaked with every move and a fan that barely worked. The cramped bathroom, the cold showers, and the lingering smell of mustiness—it had all been worth it, he thought. Justice was worth it. But now, sitting on the edge of the sagging mattress, the sound of the ceiling fan lazily spinning above, the heaviness of his loss felt unbearable. He had given everything he had, but the court had decided otherwise.

As he zipped up his bag, his hands moved mechanically, but his mind was elsewhere. He thought of his clients, Shivappa and Thimmappa, languishing in jail, their families placing all their hope in him. He thought of Rajappa, who had come to him with nothing but desperation and trust. And he thought of his own struggles—the sweat, the anxiety, the endless hours in the library, and the debates with himself over how to frame each argument. He had left no stone unturned, and yet, it hadn't been enough.

The evening prayer bell echoed from a nearby Ganesha Temple, its gentle tones breaking the stillness of the moment. Shastry paused, listening to the distant chant as it rose through the streets of Kalburgi, mingling with the soft breeze that carried the scent of street food and dust. The call seemed to stir something inside him, a quiet reminder of faith, of resilience, of hope.

He slowly knelt beside his backpack, closing his eyes, and clasped his hands together, not as a lawyer, not as an advocate, but as a man seeking answers in the face of uncertainty.

"Lord Ganapthi!" he whispered, his voice trembling with emotion. "I have done everything I could, and yet I failed. The case, the arguments, the preparation—it all feels like it has been for nothing. I have come to this city, put my heart and soul into this, but now I don't know the way forward. Please..."

Shastry paused, his voice faltering as he felt tightness in his throat. He had never been particularly religious, but at this moment, his vulnerability was laid bare. The weight of his failure bore down on him, and the uncertainty of what lay ahead felt too overwhelming to face alone.

"Please show me the light," he murmured softly. "Show me a way to conduct this trial, to bring justice where it's deserved. Help me find the strength to stand up again, to fight this battle, even when the odds seem against me. I have faith in the law, and I have faith in you. Please guide me."

For a long moment, there was only silence. Shastry remained still, his head bowed, hoping for an answer. But there was no booming voice, no divine revelation. Only the quiet sound of the fan, the distant chatter of the streets below, and the soft hum of the night beginning to fall. But somehow, that silence was enough. In his heart, a small flame of resilience flickered, a quiet reminder that the road ahead was still open, even if it seemed uncertain now.

With his prayer finished and his heart just a little lighter, Shastry hoisted his backpack onto his shoulder and made his way through the narrow streets of Kalburgi toward the train station. The streets were familiar now, but they no longer held the same promise they once did. The lodge that had become his temporary home, the courts that had challenged him—each memory weighed heavy in his mind as he walked.

When he reached the station, the train to Bengaluru stood waiting, its iron carriages illuminated by the dim lights of the platform. The whistle blew, a final call to board, and Shastry climbed inside, finding his seat by the window. The train lurched forward, and the city of Kalburgi began to slip away into the darkness behind him, the station lights flickering as they disappeared from view.

As the train picked up speed, Shastry rested his head against the cold glass of the window, watching the passing landscape blur into shadows. The moon hung low over the horizon, casting a soft silver glow over the fields and trees, but Shastry barely noticed it. His mind was still lost in the courtroom, replaying the arguments, hearing the thud of the gavel that had crushed his hopes of securing bail.

He thought of Justice Sharma—a man of such impeccable integrity and knowledge—and wondered what he could have done differently. Every moment of the arguments replayed in his mind, each word spoken by Rajshekhar Idgundi, the senior prosecutor, echoing in his ears like a taunt. He could have argued better, he told himself. He could have prepared harder, he could have... But he knew, deep down, that he had done all that he could.

As the train sped through the night, the rhythmic sound of the tracks beneath him soothed his restless mind. His eyes grew heavy, but before sleep could claim him, he whispered one last prayer, almost unconsciously.

"I will fight," he murmured, his breath fogging the window. "I won't give up."

Shastry closed his eyes, the exhaustion of the past days catching up with him, but in his heart, a small seed of hope had begun to grow again. This was only a battle—the war was far from over. The trial awaited him, and now, more than ever, he knew he had to prepare for the biggest fight of his life.

Kalburgi had been a test, a hard lesson in resilience, but as the train carried him back to Bengaluru, Shastry found comfort in the thought that failure was not the end. It was, perhaps, the beginning of something greater. As the moonlight bathed the quiet train carriage, Shastry drifted into sleep, knowing that tomorrow was a new day. And in that new day, he would find a way—he would rise again. The fight for justice was not over. It had only just begun.

COURT IS IN SESSION AT BIJAPUR

Shastry was back in Bengaluru, and the trial date for Shivappa and Thimmappa had been set. In exactly five days, he would stand before the Principal District Judge in Bijapur, arguing for the lives of his clients in a murder trial that had already tested every limit of his resilience. Yet, instead of resting or reflecting on the ordeal at the High Court in Kalburgi, Shastry threw himself head first into preparation.

The High Court Library had become his refuge, where he pored over volumes of criminal law, murder precedents, and landmark cases. But as always, the most interesting part of his preparation wasn't just the research—it was his uncanny ability to trouble the librarian.

"Shastry! Again?" the librarian, a portly old man with thick glasses, scowled as he looked at Shastry from across the desk. "You do realize it's closing time?"

Shastry looked up from his stack of books with an innocent expression, though he had already made this same request five times in the last week. "Sir, I promise this is the last time. I just need one more hour!"

The librarian let out a sigh, shaking his head as he slowly climbed the narrow ladder, grumbling under his breath. "You know, if I had a rupee for every time you asked for extra time, I could retire to a beach somewhere."

Shastry grinned as the librarian fetched another dusty volume on Section 302 of the Indian Penal Code. The old man had become something of a reluctant accomplice in Shastry's obsession, and though he pretended to be annoyed, Shastry could tell he was secretly amused by his persistence.

"Last hour," the librarian said, pointing a stubby finger in Shastry's direction, "or I'm locking you in with the books."

Shastry winked. "I wouldn't mind that, sir. The company is excellent."

With his research complete and the trial just days away, Shastry knew it was time to head back to Bijapur. But after his harrowing government bus journey the last time, Shastry wasn't taking any chances. This time, he booked a VRL sleeper bus, eager for a more comfortable ride. Still, the price of the ticket gnawed at him, so when he spotted a small quarter bottle of Old Monk at a local shop, he figured a bit of rum might ease both the financial and mental burden.

The bus was set to depart at 10:00 p.m. and as Shastry climbed into his sleeper berth, the soft hum of the engine lulling him into a sense of peace, he couldn't help but feel optimistic. He had worked tirelessly, and now, armed with his research and determination, he was ready.

By the time the bus pulled into Bijapur, Shastry was well-rested. He walked straight into the nearest lodge, a modest place, but better than his previous accommodations. After bargaining fiercely with the lodge owner, who looked like he hadn't seen a lawyer in ages, Shastry managed to secure a decent room and meals at a "throwaway price" on the condition that he would stay regularly.

"I'll be a regular visitor from now on," Shastry said, patting the owner on the back. "Good business for you, and less money for me."

The owner grinned, shaking his head. "Lawyers and their negotiation skills, eh?"

The next morning, Shastry arrived early at the Bijapur Court Complex, the courthouse standing tall in the soft morning light. He had a habit of being the first in any room he entered—a trait he had developed in law school, where it had paid off to be early. Today, he was hoping that his early arrival might pay off in building rapport with the court staff.

As he stepped inside, the court complex was just waking up. Shastry spotted the bench clerk, a gruff man with a handlebar mustache and a stern face, standing near the entrance.

Shastry approached him with a wide smile. "Good morning, sir. I'm Ramachandra Shastry, Advocate appearing on behalf of the accused in S.C. No. 143/2009."

The clerk looked him up and down, clearly unimpressed by the formality. But Shastry had learned that court clerks were the true gatekeepers of any courtroom, so he persisted with charm.

"You must be the one running the show here, sir. Without you, we're all just standing in line, aren't we?" The clerk's expression softened slightly. "You're not wrong about that," he muttered.

Shastry continued, "I just wanted to introduce myself properly, and if there's anything you need from me today, let me know. I know how busy these days get."

The clerk nodded slowly, his mustache twitching as though deciding whether or not to approve of Shastry. "Just make sure you're here on time when your case is called. The judge doesn't like delays."

Shastry grinned. "I'll be here at 11:00 a.m. sharp."

Before court commenced, Shastry made his way to the chambers of the public prosecutor, Mr. Devdas Mammani, an imposing man known for his sharp legal mind and no-nonsense demeanor. Shastry knew it was crucial to introduce himself and establish some rapport before the trial began. After all, he had learned that in the world of law, courtesy could go a long way, even if they would be on opposite sides in the courtroom.

Shastry knocked on the door of Mammani's chambers. "Come in," came the deep voice from inside.

As he stepped in, Shastry was greeted by the sight of Mr. Devdas Mammani, a large man with a stern face and an air of authority. The prosecutor glanced up from his desk, adjusting his spectacles, and fixed Shastry with a curious look.

"Ah, Mr. Shastry, I've heard about you. You're representing Shivappa and Thimmappa, aren't you?" Mammani said, not bothering to stand.

"Yes, sir," Shastry replied, a little more nervously than he intended. "I just wanted to introduce myself before we meet in court. I come from Bengalur BAR and it's my first time appearing in Bijapur."

Mammani leaned back in his chair, his expression unreadable. "First time or not, I hope you're prepared. This case isn't going to be an easy one for you. The evidence against your clients is quite damning."

Shastry smiled politely, but inside he felt the familiar tension creeping back. "I've prepared thoroughly, sir, and I'm ready to give it my all."

"Good," Mammani said, his tone softening slightly. "Just remember, in this courtroom, preparation is half the battle. The rest comes down to how well you handle the unexpected."

Shastry sat down, adjusting his black robes, trying to appear calm even though his mind was racing. "I thought it would be wise to exchange thoughts on the case, Mr. Mammani. I respect your experience, but I believe there are a few points where we might... disagree."

Finally, Mammani looked up. His piercing eyes narrowed slightly as if studying the young lawyer before him. "Oh? Disagree, you say? Well, Mr. Shastry, you're welcome to try. But experience often has a way of proving the young wrong." He leaned back, folding his arms. "So, what exactly do you find disagreeable?"

Shastry knew he was walking into a verbal sparring match, but he had come prepared. He cleared his throat, choosing his words carefully. "The prosecution's case hinges heavily on the testimonies of witnesses who saw the accused parading the heads through the village.

However, none of these witnesses saw the actual beheading. The most critical moment—the murder—is unaccounted for. Wouldn't you agree that this leaves a glaring hole in the narrative?"

Mammani's lips curled into a half-smile, though it was more condescending than warm. "Ah, the classic rookie mistake. You're focusing too much on the act itself, Shastry. In cases of this nature, it's not the act of the beheading alone that condemns your clients—it's the intent, the mens rea, that precedes it. By parading the heads through the village, your clients effectively admitted their guilt. The actus reus, is as clear as day."

Shastry felt the heat rising in his chest. He knew Mammani was trying to put him in his place, to reduce his arguments to the naiveté of a junior advocate. But he wasn't ready to give in so easily.

"With respect, sir," Shastry began, his voice gaining strength, "I don't believe this is simply about intent. The prosecution must establish a direct link between the accused and the murders. Without the weapon or the heads as material objects, the case relies solely on circumstantial evidence. And as you know, circumstantial evidence must be conclusive, not merely suggestive."

Mammani's smile faded slightly, replaced by a look of mild annoyance. He leaned forward, resting his elbows on the desk. "You're still thinking like a law student, Shastry. The courts, especially in cases of heinous crimes, are not just interested in whether we have the murder weapon or forensic evidence—though those would certainly be helpful. The courts are interested in ensuring that justice is served. And justice in this case demands that the accused face the consequences of their actions.

"You seem to think the lack of physical evidence weakens the case. But the heads were paraded. That's more than evidence—it's an admission of guilt, Mr. Shastry. You think you can poke holes in my case, but you forget that public perception plays a significant role in the courtroom, especially in a case as gruesome as this."

Shastry could feel his jaw tighten, but he kept his composure. He had to stay level-headed if he wanted to spar with someone of Mammani's stature. "Public perception shouldn't dictate legal proceedings, sir. This isn't about satisfying public outrage; it's about proving the crime in court. And right now, the prosecution has assumptions, not facts. Yes, there was a parade of heads, but who's to say the accused actually committed the beheading? What we're lacking is a direct link to the murders."

Mammani laughed softly, shaking his head. "You're bold, Shastry. I'll give you that. But boldness alone won't win a trial. I've been in this game far too long to be distracted by technicalities. The law is about interpretation as much as it is about evidence. And when you've argued as many cases as I have, you'll understand that the truth isn't always as clean as you think. Sometimes, the truth is messy—and in this case, the mess your clients left behind is undeniable.

"My job is to ensure the judge sees the bigger picture. And believe me, Judge Subramanya will. He's not going to be swayed by your nitpicking about missing heads or circumstantial evidence. He'll be looking at the totality of the case, not the tiny details you think will save your clients."

Shastry felt the weight of Mammani's words. The man was a veteran for a reason. He had seen more trials, more verdicts, more high-stakes arguments than Shastry could even imagine. But Shastry wasn't going to back down—not yet.

"You may be right about experience, Mr. Mammani," Shastry said, his voice quiet but firm. "But the law isn't about what you think the truth is. It's about what you can prove. And while you're banking on public sentiment and generalities, I'm focused on the details—the facts. It's my job to ensure that the law is upheld, not that public opinion is satisfied."

Mammani smiled again, though this time there was a flicker of something almost like respect in his eyes. He leaned back in his chair, folding his arms once more. "We'll see, Mr. Shastry. You've got spirit, I'll give you that. But spirit doesn't always win in court. I've buried many spirited lawyers with nothing more than a well-timed objection or a simple fact."

He glanced at his watch, clearly signaling the conversation was over. "I'll see you in court, Shastry. And remember—justice is the goal, not just your clients' freedom."

Shastry stood, his mind racing as he nodded and thanked Mammani for his time. As he walked out of the chamber, he couldn't shake the feeling that the senior prosecutor had rattled him more than he wanted to admit.

But beneath the doubt, there was also determination. Mammani had experience and years of victories, but Shastry had fire—and if there was one thing he had learned, it was that sometimes, fire could burn through even the most well-fortified walls.

The trial awaited, and Shastry knew it was time to fight—not just for his clients, but for his place in the legal world. Mammani may have experience, but Shastry had something to prove. By the time Shastry returned to the courtroom, the police van carrying his clients, Shivappa and Thimmappa, had just pulled into the courtyard. The clang of metal chains echoed through the air as the two brothers, both handcuffed, were led out of the van, flanked by armed police officers. Despite their grim situation, their faces lit up when they saw Shastry approaching.

"Shastry Sir!" Shivappa called out, his voice echoing in the courtyard. "How's everything? Did the bail application get through?"

Shastry shook his head, keeping his voice low but firm. "The High Court wasn't impressed. They dismissed it. But don't lose hope. We're going to fight this trial with everything we've got."

Thimmappa looked down at his feet, disappointment evident in his posture. "We've heard some big talk inside the jail," he muttered. "A lot of those big-time gangsters say they'll get us out somehow. They say the system can be worked."

Shastry's expression hardened, his voice taking on a serious tone. "Don't listen to those people. They don't know your case, and they certainly don't understand the law. I'm your lawyer, and I'll see this through. Just trust me, not them."

The two brothers nodded slowly, the weight of their situation sinking in as Shastry prepared them for the next steps.

"When the judge reads out the charges later today, I want you both to deny them. Plead not guilty, and leave the rest to me."

By 11:00 a.m., Shastry was back inside the Principal District Judge's Courtroom, waiting for the judge to arrive. The room was filled with murmurs, the buzz of lawyers shuffling papers, and the low hum of anticipation. The smell of fresh ink, old wood, and a hint of dust hung in the air as the courtroom filled up.

At the stroke of 11:00 a.m., Judge Subramanya entered the courtroom. The judge, a tall man with a stern but thoughtful expression, bowed slightly before taking his seat at the bench. The moment he sat, the entire room fell into a reverent silence.

The bench clerk, a serious-looking man with a stack of files in front of him, began calling out the cases listed in the cause list.

"S.C. No. 143/2009. State of Karnataka by Almel P.S v. Shivappa and Thimmappa."

Shastry's heart raced as the clerk called out the case. He stepped forward, giving a brief nod to the judge as the clerk informed them that the charges would be read at 3:00 p.m. after the court returned from lunch.

With a few hours to kill, Shastry found Shivappa and Thimmappa sitting quietly on a bench in the courtroom corridor, waiting for the charges to be read. He took the opportunity to sit with them, a sense of duty compelling him to spend these crucial hours preparing them mentally for what was to come.

"How's the jail treating you?" Shastry asked, trying to keep the conversation light. Thimmappa smirked. "Jail's not as bad as we thought. We've made some friends in there—professional types, real big names. They keep saying we'll walk free."

Shastry shook his head. "You can't rely on people like that. They talk big, but they don't know anything about your case. Trust me, Shivappa, Thimmappa. This is serious, and we have to approach it that way. Don't get swayed by promises from people who don't have your best interests at heart."

The brothers exchanged a glance before nodding in agreement. Shastry knew they were scared, but they needed to stay focused.

Before lunch, Shastry made one more gesture—he brought food for both Shivappa and Thimmappa. They ate together, sitting under a tree in the court complex courtyard. The simple meal was a reminder to them that, even when the world seemed to have abandoned them, Shastry was still there.

"The whole world may see you as criminals, but I see you as men who deserve a fair trial. And I'm here for you—don't forget that." The brothers smiled, their tension easing, even if just a little.

At 3:00 p.m., the courtroom was filled with tension as Judge Subramanya re-entered and resumed his seat. The courtroom buzzed with anticipation as the clerk rose to call the case.

"S.C.No.:143/2009. State of Karnataka v. Shivappa and Thimmappa."

Shastry stood up as the judge prepared to read the charges. The air felt thick with importance. As the clerk handed over the charge sheet, Judge Subramanya's voice was calm but commanding as he read out the charges of double murder.

"Shivappa and Thimmappa, you are charged with the murder of Mohan and Beerappa under Section 302 of the IPC. How do you plead?"

Shastry glanced at his clients, giving them a firm nod, signaling them to follow his instructions.

"Not guilty, Sir," Shivappa and Thimmappa said in unison, their voices steady despite the anxiety they must have felt.

The judge gave a nod of acknowledgment. "Very well. Let the trial proceed. This Court will ensure that the matter is disposed of quickly. We will have day to day hearings. Issue summons to CW1 to CW18." The judge then turned to the Investigation Officer Kalappa who was present. "Make sure you bring all the witnesses tomorrow securely. Provide all necessary protection to them."

As the court session ended for the day, Shastry felt a wave of emotions wash over him. The journey had been long, filled with doubt and moments of despair. Yet, here he was—fighting for justice, standing by two men who had been abandoned by society. He was their only hope, and he would not let them down.

As he left the courthouse that evening, the setting sun bathed Bijapur in a warm, golden glow. Shastry looked up at the sky, whispering a silent prayer once more, not for himself, but for the strength to see this trial through to the end.

He knew the battle was far from over, but for now, the fight for justice had begun in earnest.

The next morning, Ramachandra Shastry arrived at the Bijapur court complex early, as usual. The cool morning air had not done much to calm his nerves, and the weight of the day's events hung heavily on his shoulders. Today was the day he would have to cross-examine witnesses for the first time in his career, and the stakes couldn't be higher. Shivappa and Thimmappa's freedom, and perhaps their very lives, depended on his performance in court. He knew every legal principle by heart—evidence law, cross-examination strategies, everything. But knowing it in theory and executing it under the stern gaze of Judge Subramanya were two different things.

Shastry nervously shuffled through his case papers, his mind racing. He couldn't afford to make a mistake. One slip in his questioning could lead to disaster—a conviction for double murder.

Just as he was about to drown in his anxiety, the door to the courtroom swung open, and in marched Kalappa, the investigating officer for the case. His face, usually one of casual indifference, was now twisted with panic. Shastry noticed him immediately.

Judge Subramanya entered the courtroom soon after, his expression as stormy as the monsoon clouds that loomed outside. He took his seat on the bench and wasted no time in starting the proceedings. His voice was calm, but there was an unmistakable edge of irritation.

"Kalappa!" he thundered, turning his gaze toward the visibly nervous investigating officer. "Where are the witnesses that you were ordered to secure?"

Kalappa, a usually overconfident man, fidgeted like a schoolboy caught in trouble. "My Lord, I had sent a constable to bring them from the village, but—"

"But?" Judge Subramanya's eyebrows shot up, his patience clearly thinning. "Do you mean to tell me that you've sent one constable to bring 18 witnesses, and neither he nor the witnesses have arrived?"

Kalappa gulped visibly, his hands twisting nervously in front of him. "Yes, My Lord. The village is 120 kilometers away, and the constable has not returned yet."

The judge's face grew red with frustration. He banged his fist lightly on the bench, his voice rising in anger. "This is unacceptable! How many times must I remind you that this is a court of law, not a village gathering? The court had ordered the presence of these witnesses today, and your negligence has led to a complete waste of judicial time!"

Shastry, watching the scene unfold, sensed anopportunity. He sprang to his feet, his nerves now replaced by a sudden burst of courage.

"My Lord," he began, his voice more confident than he felt, "this entire situation is an example of the lackadaisical approach of the police in handling this case! I have traveled all the way from Bengaluru for this trial, and every day that goes by without progress creates a bigger hole in my pocket. We are talking about the lives of two men here, and the police seem to be taking this as a joke!"

Judge Subramanya turned his gaze to Shastry, his expression softening slightly but still stern. "Mr. Shastry, I understand your frustration. Believe me, I am not pleased with the lack of coordination from the police. However, this is not my problem. You, as counsel, should have thought carefully before taking on such a case. Trials are unpredictable, and delays are part of the process."

Shastry clenched his jaw, realizing that despite the judge's understanding, there was no real sympathy for his predicament. "But, My Lord," he pressed on, "surely there must be some accountability for this kind of negligence. My clients—"

"Enough, Mr. Shastry," Judge Subramanya interrupted, though his tone was not as harsh. "I sympathize with your position, but the law moves at its own pace. You will have to face the repercussions of these delays. I am adjourning the case until tomorrow."

The gavel came down with a resounding thud, signaling the end of the day's session. Shastry sighed, feeling a mixture of relief and disappointment. He had hoped to get through at least one cross-examination today, but it seemed fate had other plans.

With the rest of the day free and his courtroom frustrations temporarily set aside, Shastry decided to explore the historical wonders of Bijapur. He wasn't one to waste time, and with the court adjourned until the next day, he figured he might as well learn something about the city while he waited.

His first stop was the Gol Gumbaz, the most famous monument in Bijapur. As he walked up to the massive structure, he couldn't help but be awestruck by its sheer size. The dome, the second largest in the world after St. Peter's Basilica in Rome, loomed over him like a giant in stone. He marveled at the architecture, built in 1656, housing the tomb of Sultan Mohammed Adil Shah.

The famous whispering gallery inside the dome was his next destination. He stood at one end and whispered a few words, only to hear them echoed clearly on the other side of the gallery—a phenomenon that never failed to fascinate tourists. He couldn't help but chuckle as he tested the acoustics, trying to make sense of how such ancient architecture could carry sound so perfectly.

Next, he made his way to the Barah Kamaan, a half-finished mausoleum intended to be the resting place of Ali

Adil Shah II. The twelve arches (hence the name "Barah Kamaan") stood like sentinels of history, unfinished yet still magnificent in their incomplete beauty. As Shastry wandered through the arches, he couldn't help but feel a sense of connection to his own journey—incomplete, but filled with promise. Much like these arches, he still had much to learn, but he was standing tall despite the challenges.

The Ibrahim Rauza, another monument built during the reign of the Adil Shahi dynasty, was next on his list. Known as the inspiration for the Taj Mahal, the structure was a symbol of balance, symmetry, and grace. Shastry spent the afternoon marveling at its intricate carvings, the gardens surrounding it offering a serene escape from the stress of the courtroom.

After a day of exploring, Shastry returned to the lodge feeling surprisingly light. He had spent the day not thinking about the trial, and the historical richness of Bijapur had provided a much-needed distraction from the pressures of his profession.

That evening, he opted for a light dinner at a small local eatery. The menu was simple—jolada rotti (sorghum flatbread), enne badanekayi (stuffed eggplant), and a small plate of mirchi bhajji. The meal was delicious, a reminder that even in small towns, the food could be as rich as the history.

He sat there, lost in thought, savoring each bite. The conversations from the nearby tables floated through the air, the chatter of locals and the occasional clink of metal plates creating a pleasant backdrop to his quiet meal. It was a stark contrast to the intensity of his day, and for a brief moment, Shastry allowed himself to forget about the trial.

As the evening drew to a close, Shastry retired to his room, the excitement of the day slowly giving way to the nervous anticipation of what tomorrow would bring. The trial was looming, and though the delay had bought him some time, he knew that the real test of his skills was yet to come.

Lying on the small, firm bed in the lodge, Shastry stared up at the ceiling, the familiar sound of the ceiling fan whirring softly in the background. He thought back to the monuments he had visited that day, especially the unfinished arches of the Barah Kamaan.

"Maybe I'm like those arches," he mused to himself, "unfinished, but still standing. Still strong." With that thought, Shastry closed his eyes, ready for whatever challenges the next day would bring.

The day had finally arrived. Shastry was back in the Bijapur Court Complex, nervous but resolute. Today, after the endless delays, the cross-examinations were scheduled to begin. The constable had finally managed to secure all 18 witnesses, as ordered by the court, and Shastry's nerves were in overdrive. He knew the importance of today's proceedings—one misstep in his questioning, and Shivappa and Thimmappa's fate would be sealed.

Inside the courtroom, the usual hum of activity filled the air, but Shastry's mind was racing. Did the constable really manage to bring all 18 witnesses? What kind of testimony would they give? He had spent nights preparing for this moment, going over every legal principle, every tactic of cross-examination. But as he waited, his anxiety gnawed at him.

Just as Shastry was lost in his thoughts, he heard a familiar voice outside the courtroom. It was the constable, excited and animated, recounting his heroic ordeal to Kalappa, the Investigating Officer.

"Sir, you won't believe what I've been through!" the constable puffed, wiping sweat from his brow, as if he had just returned from a battlefield. "I had to travel all the way to that godforsaken village—120 kilometers! You know how these villagers are, right? I had to beg, plead, and even bribe them with some tea and snacks just to get them to leave their fields. And don't even get me started on the vehicle breakdown! We were stuck in the mud for an hour."

The court staff, lawyers, and even Shastry had been skeptical that Kalappa would be able to gather so many witnesses from a remote village, but here they were. Kalappa was practically strutting through the court corridors, a smile of victory plastered across his face. The constable, on the other hand, looked exhausted, as if he had been through a battlefield.

Kalappa, always quick to take credit for anything remotely successful, smiled proudly as if it were his own plan that had ensured the witnesses' arrival. "Well done! I'll be sure to mention your name to the judge when he asks. It's a big day today—18 witnesses! That's not something the court sees every day."

Tales Of Lawyer Ramachandra Shastry

"Thank you, sir," the constable said, puffing out his chest. "But, sir, between you and me, these villagers... well, they're a bit hard to manage. Some of them didn't even want to come, and others have no idea what's going on. One man thought he was here for a wrestling match! Another asked if he could sell his goat outside the court!" The constable chuckled nervously, clearly aware that controlling such a group would be a challenge.

Kalappa grinned, clapping the constable on the back. "Don't worry, we'll get through it. Let's take them to Mammani's chambers and have him prepare them."

Devdas Mammani, the senior public prosecutor, was sitting in his chambers, meticulously preparing for the day. His chambers were a mess of case files, notes, and law books strewn across the table, but his mind was focused on one thing: winning the trial. He had 18 witnesses to guide through testimony today, and he knew it wouldn't be easy. These were simple villagers, most of whom had likely never seen the inside of a courtroom, let alone testified in a double murder case.

As Kalappa and the constable shepherded the witnesses into Mammani's chambers, the prosecutor immediately sensed trouble. The group of villagers looked bewildered, their eyes wide with confusion and nervousness. One elderly woman clutched a bag of peanuts, chewing noisily, while a middle-aged man in a torn dhoti stared blankly at the wall.

Mammani sighed deeply, feeling the pressure mount. "Alright, everyone, listen carefully. When you're called to the stand, you'll be asked about the parade of heads you saw in the village. Just tell the truth, don't get nervous, and—"

Before he could finish, one of the men raised his hand. "Sir, is there any chance we can finish quickly? I left my goats untied at home. They'll wander off if I'm not back by evening."

Another woman piped up, "And my son's getting married next week, sir. I need to buy bangles from the market before sunset."

Mammani rubbed his temples, his composure starting to crack. He had dealt with difficult witnesses before, but this was turning into a circus.

"I understand you all have important things to do, but this is a court case. A serious matter! You need to be focused."

Just as he was about to continue, a third villager spoke up. "Sir, the bus ride was bumpy. Is there any food here? I'm feeling a little faint."

Mammani's frustration reached a boiling point. These villagers were completely unprepared, and there was no telling how they would behave on the stand. He glanced nervously at the clock. Shastry would be cross-examining them soon, and though the young lawyer lacked experience, Mammani couldn't shake the feeling that Shastry might pull a rabbit out of the hat during cross-examination.

"Just stick to the facts," Mammani said, his voice firm but strained. "And please, for the love of law, do not talk about goats, bangles, or food in front of the judge."

The villagers nodded, but Mammani wasn't convinced. This was going to be a long day.

At exactly 11:00 a.m., Judge Subramanya entered the courtroom, punctual as always. His robes billowed slightly as he made his way to the bench, and the entire room fell into a respectful hush. Today, the judge had a clear agenda: he was determined to complete the evidence of 18 witnesses in one go.

As usual, the court clerk began calling out the cases from the cause list, working through the routine matters. When S.C. No. 143/2009 was called at Item No. 56, Shastry, Kalappa, and Mammani all stood to attention. The judge glanced at the list of cases before him, sighed, and announced, "This case will be taken up after the cause list is over. We'll deal with the witnesses then."

Shastry felt his stomach twist into knots. He had been nervously biting his nails all morning, and now, with the delay, he was on the verge of chewing his fingers. He watched as Judge Subramanya meticulously worked through the list of cases, one by one. The minutes seemed to crawl by, and by 12:15 p.m., Shastry was a ball of anxiety.

Finally, the court clerk called out again, "S.C. No. 143/2009. State of Karnataka v. Shivappa and Thimmappa."

Shastry stood, his heart pounding in his chest. Kalappa and his constable rushed forward, but something was wrong. Kalappa's face, which had been glowing with pride earlier, was now pale.

"My Lord," the constable stammered, looking like he wanted to melt into the floor. "The... the witnesses, sir. They're missing!"

The courtroom erupted in confusion.

"What do you mean, missing?" Judge Subramanya thundered, his usually calm demeanor shattered by the news.

Kalappa stepped forward, his voice shaking. "My Lord, we had all 18 witnesses here this morning. But now, they've... they've disappeared. We can't find them anywhere."

"Disappeared?" The judge's face turned crimson with anger. "Are you telling me you've lost 18 witnesses in the span of two hours? What is this—some kind of joke?"

Kalappa and the constable stammered, desperately trying to explain. "My Lord, they must have... they must have wandered off!" Kalappa offered weakly.

Judge Subramanya slammed his fist on the bench. "This is utter incompetence! I adjourned all the other matters today to record the evidence of these witnesses, and now they're missing? Kalappa, you've crossed every limit of incompetence, and I'm seriously contemplating issuing a recommendation for your suspension!"

The courtroom was in chaos. Lawyers whispered among themselves, and the constable looked like he was about to faint. Shivappa and Thimmappa, sitting in the back of the courtroom, seemed entirely unamused by the debacle. They exchanged bored glances, clearly accustomed to the bureaucratic comedy unfolding around them.

Shastry, who had been biting his nails for hours, now saw a chance. He quickly rose to his feet, his voice calm but decisive. "My Lord, in light of today's developments, I respectfully request a 15-day adjournment. I have pending court work in Bengaluru, and it seems we'll need more time to secure the witnesses."

Judge Subramanya, still fuming, turned to Shastry. "Mr. Shastry, I understand your request, and while I am extremely frustrated by the incompetence displayed today, I will grant your adjournment." He turned back to Kalappa, his voice cold. "But Kalappa, mark my words—if all 38 witnesses are not present on the next date of hearing, I will issue strictures against you and your entire team. Do I make myself clear?"

Kalappa nodded furiously, looking like a mancondemned.

"The matter is adjourned," Judge Subramanya declared, banging the gavel.

Amid the flurry of confusion inside the courtroom, Shastry's eyes caught something unsettling—something that immediately triggered the lawyer's sixth sense. As the courtroom buzzed with Kalappa's fumbling explanations and the judge's rising fury, Shastry's focus shifted entirely to his clients, Shivappa and Thimmappa.

There it was—Shivappa, sitting casually, wore an expression that didn't match the gravity of the situation. It wasn't just any grin; it was a wild, evilish grin, the kind that hinted at a secret victory only he understood. Thimmappa, in contrast, had kept his head bowed the entire time, concealing something, his face hidden under a shadow of guilt and tension.

Shastry's pulse quickened. Something was amiss. Big time! As soon as the court adjourned and the trio of Shivappa, Thimmappa, and Kalappa were making their way out of the courtroom, Shastry's instincts kicked in. He felt the cold grip of suspicion tightening around his thoughts. He had a gnawing feeling that the absence of the 18 witnesses wasn't some mere administrative blunder—it was far more calculated.

Outside the courtroom, the chaos continued, with constables gathering their belongings, lawyers discussing upcoming cases, and Kalappa, still nursing his bruised ego after the judge's reprimand, muttering to his colleague.

Shastry saw his moment. "Kalappa!" he called, keeping his voice neutral, though the urgency was undeniable. Kalappa turned, his expression bewildered after the court's scolding.

"What now, Shastry?" Kalappa muttered, still flustered.

"I need to speak to Shivappa. Alone." Shastry's voice was steady, though the unease gnawed at his insides.

Kalappa raised an eyebrow. "Alone, huh? You sure you're not going to lose him? Judge Subramanya might hang me if these two disappear on my watch."

Shastry's lips twitched into a forced smile. "I promise not to lose them. Besides, after today, I think they know better than to run."

Kalappa hesitated for a beat, then sighed, "Alright, but if you lose them, you're on your own!" He winked half-heartedly before turning his back to deal with some paperwork.

The moment Kalappa's back was turned, Shastry acted Like a lion sensing weakness in its prey, and grabbed Shivappa by the collar and swiftly cornered him against the courthouse wall with surprising force. The nearby constables and lawyers barely noticed the sudden movement, too preoccupied with their own affairs. The once-smug Shivappa was now pinned to the cold stone wall, his evil grin wiped away, replaced by shock and terror.

"Boli Magne! Ello Saakshigalu?" Shastry growled through gritted teeth, his voice low but brimming with fury. (Son of a… Where are the witnesses?)

Shivappa's eyes widened in panic. The audacity of Shastry's strength, both mental and physical, was something he hadn't anticipated. Thimmappa, standing a few feet away, froze in place, his mouth slightly open in shock, his hands twitching nervously as if unsure whether to intervene.

For a fleeting moment, Shivappa seemed genuinely scared. He had seen men break in interrogation rooms, but here, under Shastry's relentless grip, he was both rattled by the lawyer's intensity and stunned by his raw physical power. It was as if Shastry had transformed into something primal—his presence overwhelming, his strength comparable to both a lion's rage and an elephant's force.

"Let me go!" Shivappa pleaded, his voice cracking under the weight of fear. "I'll admit everything! Just let go!"

Shastry held him there for another second, his eyes locked onto Shivappa's, daring him to lie. His mind raced, but his body remained perfectly still, his grip firm. He was in control, and he knew it. Then, just as quickly, Shastry released him, taking a deep breath to calm himself.

Thimmappa, sensing the tension in the air, rushed over. "Sir, please! Let's talk. We'll explain everything. Please, don't make a scene here."

Shastry straightened up, smoothing the creases on his robe. He could feel the eyes of the courthouse staff glancing at them from a distance, but he didn't care. "Fine." His voice was firm, but a crack of suspicion lingered in it. "Let's take this to the canteen. I need a cigarette."

The court canteen was bustling with activity, filled with litigants, constables, and a handful of lawyers grabbing quick cups of tea between hearings. The smell of stale samosas and over-brewed chai filled the air as Shastry led the two brothers to an isolated table in the corner. He lit a cigarette, taking a deep drag before glaring at Shivappa.

"Now talk."

Shivappa and Thimmappa exchanged uneasy glances before Shivappa finally began. "It wasn't supposed to go this far, sir," Shivappa muttered, looking down at the table. "I made some... friends in jail. Some big people. They said they could handle everything for us."

Shastry exhaled a cloud of smoke, his patience thinning. "Friends? What friends?"

Shivappa fumbled inside his shirt pocket, pulling out a crumpled piece of paper with a scrawled phone number. He slid it across the table. "They call him 'Paapa.' He said he'd help us get out of this mess. No witnesses, no case. That's what he promised."

Shastry's heart sank, though his face remained calm. This was bigger than he thought. "So Paapa's men... they took the witnesses?"

Shivappa nodded nervously. "They came this morning, dressed like election workers. Promised the villagers food, liquor, 100 rupees each. The villagers didn't think twice—they jumped into the tempo like it was a festival. Paapa's men drove them to some place outside town. Their plan is to beat them up, scare them and tell them if they testified, they'd kill their families."

Shastry's cigarette trembled between his fingers, but he quickly steadied his hand. "And where are they now?"

"I don't know!" All I know is that there is a panchaythi happening at Bhagyawanthi temple by 7:30 p.m. today at my village which is 120 km away," Thimmappa chimed in, his voice quiet. "Paapa's men said they'd bring them there when the time's right. Said it's taken care of."

Shastry took another deep drag of his cigarette, the weight of the situation pressing down on him. He flicked the ash into the tray and crushed the cigarette under his thumb. "I need to talk to this Paapa.

Without wasting any time, Shastry excused himself and headed to a nearby payphone. He dialed the number on the crumpled piece of paper, and after two rings, a gravelly voice answered.

"Yeah?"

"This is Shastry. I'm the lawyer for Shivappa and Thimmappa."

A pause, then the voice said, "I was wondering when you'd call. Meet me at the Bhagyawanthi temple by 6:00 p.m. I'll be there. And bring nothing but yourself."

The line went dead.

It was just after noon when Shastry's phone rang, its shrill tone cutting through the silence of his office. He had been staring blankly at his papers, trying to make sense of the whirlwind of events that had unfolded since the case began, but nothing had prepared him for the message he was about to receive.

"It's Paapa," the voice on the other end was cold and direct. "You want to win this case, right? I've left you a little something. There's a motorcycle waiting for you near the old ruins at Barah Kamaan. A Bajaj Pulsar 150cc. Take it, and make sure you're at the village by 5:00 p.m."

Before Shastry could respond, the line went dead. He stared at the phone for a moment, unsure of what to think. Why a bike? Why this village? Paapa's cryptic instructions gnawed at him, but he had no choice. The plan was already in motion.

Shastry quickly packed up his belongings and made his way to the Barah Kamaan, one of Bijapur's oldest and most mysterious monuments. The crumbling twelve arches stood like sentinels, watching over the past as if guarding the secrets of centuries gone by. The area was mostly deserted, save for a few curious tourists and the occasional local loitering about. In the shadow of one of the arches, there it was—a gleaming Bajaj Pulsar 150cc, its black paint reflecting the midday sun. The bike looked brand new, its body muscular and sleek, and as Shastry approached, he saw a small note taped to the handlebars written in Kannada.

"*Laawyer Shashtrigaligagi..... Petrol full ide.... Enjoy maadi*" .... "(For Lawyer Shastry. Petrol tank full. Enjoy the ride)."

Shastry's lips curled into a slight smile. A Pulsar 150cc. It had always been his dream bike. The sheer power of the machine, the speed, the control—it was everything he had ever wanted in a motorcycle. He swung a leg over the seat, gripping the handlebars, and turned the key. The engine roared to life, its deep hum sending a thrill through his veins. Paapa had kept his promise—the fuel tank was indeed full.

But before hitting the road, Shastry decided to grab a light meal at a nearby roadside eatery. He parked the bike and strolled over to a small, humble khanavali. The smell of sizzling masala girmits and fresh chapatis filled the air, and Shastry couldn't resist. He ordered a simple meal, nothing too heavy—a couple of chapatis, some dal, and a side handful of raw onions. As he ate, he felt the weight of the day's impending journey start to lift. The simplicity of the meal grounded him, the earthy flavors of the food reminding him of home, of simpler times.

After finishing his meal, Shastry lit a cigarette, inhaling deeply. The first drag brought a wave of calm over him, the tension in his shoulders easing as the smoke curled lazily into the air. He stood by the roadside, watching the traffic pass by, the hum of life going on around him, oblivious to the gravity of the situation he was about to ride into.

By 2:00 p.m., Shastry was back on the Pulsar, the sun high in the sky as he set off on his journey. The 150-kilometer ride ahead of him would take him deep into the countryside, through villages, fields, and winding roads that stretched far beyond the bustling city of Bijapur. But for the moment, it was just Shastry, the open road, and his bike.

The Pulsar roared as he accelerated, the wind whipping past him, carrying away the dust and the noise of the city. This was freedom. The bike responded to his every touch, the engine purring beneath him, ready for anything. Shastry leaned into the curves of the road, his body moving in sync with the machine, feeling the thrill of the ride with every mile that passed. The open highway stretched out before him, endless and inviting.

As he cruised along, the vast, golden fields of sugarcane swayed gently in the breeze on either side of the road. The occasional bullock cart trundled along, and villagers waved curiously as the sleek Pulsar zipped past. The landscape shifted from dry, rocky terrain to stretches of lush greenery, a stark contrast to the ancient city he had left behind.

By 3:30 p.m., Shastry had covered a good distance, but the heat of the sun and the constant roar of the bike had begun to wear him down. He pulled over at a small roadside shop, more of a shack than a store, where an old man sat chewing on betel leaf, his teeth stained red from years of indulgence.

Shastry parked the bike and lit another cigarette, leaning against the Pulsar as he took in the sights and sounds of rural Karnataka. A group of boys, curious about the shiny motorcycle, gathered around at a safe distance, whispering among themselves. Shastry offered them a nod, but his mind was focused elsewhere.

Inside the shop, the old man beckoned him over. "Gutka, sir?" he asked, holding up a brightly colored packet.

Shastry hesitated for a moment. He hadn't chewed gutka in years, not since his college days, but something about the long road ahead made him crave its sharp, bitter taste. He accepted the packet, tore it open, and slipped a pinch of the Tobacco-Limestone-Areca-Masala laced mixture into his mouth. The familiar burn hit his senses, and for a brief moment, Shastry was transported back to his youth—back to the carefree days when the world seemed smaller, less complicated.

He spat out the remnants, washed it down with a cold soda from the shop, and took one last drag from his cigarette. The road called to him, and there was still a long way to go.

By 4:30 p.m., the landscape began to change once again. The sun was starting its slow descent, casting long shadows across the road. Shastry felt a sense of calm wash over him as he neared the end of his journey. The village was close now, just a few kilometers away, and the road had narrowed to a dusty path lined with ancient trees. The Pulsar, though sleek and powerful, now felt almost out of place in this rustic setting, but Shastry didn't mind.

With the wind still in his hair and the smell of earth and fields all around him, Shastry smiled. For a brief moment, the case, the witnesses, and even Paapa were forgotten. There was only the road, the ride, and the sense of freedom that came with it.

By the time 5:30 p.m. rolled around, Shastry found himself at the edge of the village, the Bhagyawanthi temple looming in the distance. The small homes were scattered across the landscape, smoke rising from cooking fires, and the faint sound of a distant temple bell echoed through the air.

He parked the Pulsar, admiring the beast of a bike before taking off his helmet. The ride had been everything he'd dreamed of—powerful, exhilarating, and strangely peaceful.

But now, the real task lay ahead. Shastry took a deep breath, lit one last cigarette, and exhaled slowly, watching the smoke dissipate into the warm evening air. The village was waiting. And so was the truth he had come to uncover.

As Shastry rolled into the village, the roar of his Pulsar 150cc still echoing in the distance, he was immediately greeted by an unexpected crowd of villagers. The moment he removed his helmet and dismounted the bike, there was an almost reverential hush. Before he could process the situation, people began to approach him—men, women, children—each with offerings.

A young boy shyly handed him a brass pot full of fresh sugarcane juice, its sweet aroma mixing with the earthy smell of the village. An elderly man approached him with a pot of water, gesturing for him to freshen up. Women with vibhuti and kumkum approached him, gently smearing his forehead, marking him as if he were more than a mere lawyer—a demi-god who had come to dispense justice.

"What's all this?" Shastry murmured to himself, his brows knitting together as flowers were placed at his feet.

It was overwhelming. In a span of moments, he had gone from lawyer to something much more divine in the eyes of the villagers. There was a palpable energy, a collective expectation that he was there for something greater than he had ever imagined.

Shastry knew something was amiss—this was not the ordinary reception one expected in a village where tempers flared and lives hung in the balance. They were preparing him for something.

"Please, come with us," a man whispered, bowing slightly. He motioned toward an ancient Baobab tree at the edge of the village. Beneath its gnarled roots sat a small idol, barely visible through the leaves and offerings at its base. This was Bhagyawanthi! the village DEITY! Revered as a form of Durga, the goddess of fortune and destiny. The villagers believed she could bless her devotees with Bhagya—good luck, prosperity, and fortune.

Shastry hesitated but allowed himself to be led toward the shrine. As they reached the Baobab tree, the villagers gently, but firmly, guided him to sit next to the idol, a place of honor. The weight of their expectations pressed on him. He wasn't just a lawyer in their eyes anymore—he was a witness, a part of their ritual.

Just as Shastry was settling into his uncomfortable role by the idol, a tempo rolled into the village, kicking up dust in its wake. The sight that followed nearly took the breath out of Shastry's lungs.

The 18 missing witnesses tumbled out of the vehicle, their faces bruised, bodies covered in cuts and welts. They had clearly been beaten—black and blue, every one of them. The tempo door slid open with a creak, and the villagers began to gather in silence, watching the beaten men and women with a strange mixture of pity and expectation.

As the crowd murmured, out from the shadows appeared the local landlord, his face as bruised as the witnesses, his once-pristine white dhoti now smeared with dirt. His eyes flickered with both fear and submission, and it was clear that he too had been visited by the same miscreants.

Shastry's stomach twisted in knots. He felt a deep unease settle over him as the figures continued to emerge from the growing twilight of the village.

Then, in a moment of complete absurdity, Paapa appeared.

Paapa—the gangster Shastry had only heard of in whispers—walked into the scene with an air of authority that was both commanding and terrifying. He didn't address the villagers. Instead, his eyes went straight to Shastry, sitting by the Bhagyawanthi idol.

Paapa approached slowly, and in a gesture that shocked Shastry to his core, the feared gangster bowed before him. "As per the orders of Goddess Bhagyawanthi, we obey."

The air was thick with tension. Shastry felt the weight of every eye in the village upon him. What order? What was happening?

For a brief moment, an unsettling silence enveloped the village. Even the trees seemed to have stopped rustling in the breeze, as if the world itself was holding its breath. Then, from within the crowd, a frail old woman stepped forward. Her eyes, which had been dull and vacant, suddenly gleamed with a manic intensity. Without warning, she began to shake violently, her arms flailing as if controlled by an unseen force.

Shastry's blood ran cold.

The woman's body twisted and contorted, her movements jerky and unnatural. Her voice, once a frail whisper, now boomed through the air as she screamed in a voice not her own, "Bhagyawanthi!"

The villagers gasped. Shastry's heart pounded in his chest. Was she... possessed? The woman moved in a circle, her arms raised to the heavens, performing a frenzied tandava—a violent, primal dance that seemed to call upon forces far beyond human comprehension.

Her eyes locked onto Shastry's, and for a fleeting second, he felt as though he was gazing into the very heart of Goddess Durga!! His body tensed, the fight-or-flight response kicking in, but he was rooted to the spot, stunned, petrified and terrified.

The possessed woman stopped her dance abruptly and began to speak, her voice resonating with an authority that didn't seem human. "Two women were raped. Their honors snatched due to lust! We have committed sin to our mother, Bhagyawanthi!"

The crowd went deathly silent.

The woman's eyes flashed with divine fire as she continued. "Bhagyawanthi herself commanded her sons to carry out the punishment—chop off the heads of Mohan and Beerappa with *Kattega* as retribution! Shivappa and Thimmappa are mere puppets, carrying out orders from the divine."

Shastry's breath caught in his throat. So that's how the village saw it. Shivappa and Thimmappa weren't killers—they were vessels of justice. But what was being presented to him wasn't law. It was something much more primal, something beyond any legal framework Shastry had ever known.

The woman continued, her voice softer now but no less powerful. "Those who stand against Shivappa and Thimmappa will meet the same fate as Mohan and Beerappa!! Bhagyawanthi demands that the fathers of the dead men offer jaggery to the father of the killers Shivappa, and Thimmappa—as a peace ritual."

The landlord, still visibly bruised, stepped forward slowly, his face a mask of defeat. In his trembling hand, he held a small ball of jaggery—the sweet offering of peace. He approached Rajappa's father, a man as worn as the land he tilled, and placed the jaggery into his mouth.

The exchange was silent but filled with the weight of centuries of tradition and superstition. Shastry watched, stunned, as the ritual unfolded before his eyes.

After the ritual was completed, the old woman, still possessed by the spirit of Bhagyawanthi, turned to Shastry, her voice echoing in the twilight. "Lawyer Shastry is witness to my words! No one will speak in court. I AM BHAGYAVANTHI!"

With that final decree, she collapsed onto the ground, the life drained from her body as the divine presence left her. The villagers quickly gathered around her, whispering prayers, but Shastry remained frozen by the idol.

One by one, the 38 witnesses fell to their knees before the deity and before Shastry, their faces etched with the fear and reverence that only a divine judgment could inspire.

The sun had almost set now, casting long shadows over the village. Shastry sat beside the Bhagyawanthi idol, his mind reeling. This wasn't just about the law anymore. It was about ancient beliefs, a justice that transcended the courts, a justice handed down by a goddess that the villagers held in awe and fear.

He wasn't sure what to do next. The trial still awaited him in court, but now the stakes were far greater. What did it mean to be a lawyer in a world where gods and goddesses had already passed their judgment?

As the villagers dispersed, Shastry remained, staring into the distance, knowing that his battle was far from over. A new chapter in this case was about to begin.

And Bhagyawanthi, it seemed, had already written the next part of the story.

The night had fallen quietly upon the village, with the last rays of the sun casting long shadows over the Bhagyawanthi temple, where Shastry sat next to the idol of the goddess. The events of the day had left him emotionally drained, but the weight of what he had witnessed—the ritual, the possessed old woman's words, and the decree of Bhagyawanthi—still clung to him. He had come to this village a lawyer, but the things he had experienced were far beyond any legal battle.

As the stars twinkled above in the wide, unblemished sky, Shastry felt a strange pull—a deep connection to the deity that stood before him. In his exhaustion, he decided to stay the night next to the idol. Bhagyawanthi was no longer just a village deity in his eyes—she had taken on a form much more personal, almost maternal. For reasons beyond logic, he felt like a child returning to his mother, seeking solace after a storm.

The stone platform beside the Baobab tree was rough and cold, but it didn't matter. Shastry curled up next to the deity as if it were a protective shield, the goddess's presence filling him with an unusual sense of comfort. It was like sleeping in his mother's lap—a place of safety, warmth, and unconditional love. His head gently rested against the stone, and in moments, his eyes fluttered closed. He drifted off into a deep, dreamless sleep, undisturbed by the chaos of the world around him.

In the early hours of dawn, the village lay cloaked in soft mist, the Baobab tree standing like a guardian in the grey light. At around 4:30 a.m., a gentle voice broke through Shastry's peaceful slumber.

"Maga, Elu." (Son, wake up.)

Shastry stirred, his eyelids fluttering open. His body felt heavy with sleep, but the voice was so calm, so nurturing, that it beckoned him to consciousness. As his eyes focused in the dim light emanating from the lamp lit next to the Deity, he saw the old woman—the same woman who had been possessed by Bhagyawanthi the night before. But now, she was different. She was no longer wild with divine fury; instead, she stood before him with a serene, almost maternal aura.

In her hand, she held a clay pot full of fresh cow's milk. The pot was slightly warm, steam rising gently from the opening. Her eyes, though worn with age, were soft and full of kindness. She knelt beside Shastry, holding the pot out to him.

"Kudi, maga. It will give you strength."

Shastry, still groggy from sleep, instinctively reached for the pot. The moment the warm milk touched his lips, he felt a wave of energy and warmth rush through his body. He drank deeply, the taste pure and sweet, filling him with an unusual sense of vitality. It was as though every drop carried the blessing of Bhagyawanthi herself, rejuvenating him from within.

As he finished the last gulp, the old woman smiled warmly. "The goddess will always be by your side, Shastry. You must leave now, before the sun rises. Go back to Bijapur. The path ahead of you will be difficult, but you are not alone. Remember this—Bhagyawanthi is with you, wherever you go."

Shastry nodded, still feeling the exuberance the milk had brought him. His mind was clearer, sharper. He felt a deep sense of gratitude and humility wash over him. This wasn't just another case now—it was something larger, something deeply spiritual. He bowed his head to the woman, thanking her silently, and with a quiet nod, she stepped back, watching as Shastry prepared to leave.

The early morning air was cool as Shastry mounted the Pulsar 150cc. The bike rumbled to life, and with one last glance at the Bhagyawanthi temple, he revved the engine and sped away from the village, the mist parting in his wake.

The road ahead was long—120 kilometers of open rural highway stretched before him, but the journey felt different now. Shastry's mind was clear, his heart light. The ride that had once been about the case, about strategy, was now something else entirely. It was a pilgrimage. Every turn, every gust of wind that hit his face, was a reminder of the goddess's presence, of the strength she had bestowed upon him.

As the bike roared along the countryside, the landscape unfurled before him in all its beauty—fields of sugarcane, the occasional bullock cart, and the quiet hum of the early morning world. The journey was solitary, but Shastry didn't feel alone. The goddess was with him, her invisible hand guiding him back to Bijapur.

At one point, Shastry pulled over by a small roadside tea stall. The sun was just beginning to rise, casting a golden glow over the horizon. He lit a cigarette, leaning against the bike as he inhaled deeply, watching the smoke curl lazily into the cool morning air. The taste of the smoke mingled with the earthy smell of the morning dew, and for the first time in days, Shastry felt at peace.

He spotted a small gutka stall nearby and decided to indulge in an old habit. He slipped the bitter tobacco into his mouth, thesharp taste instantly reminding him of late nights spent cramming legal books and early mornings spent arguing mock cases.

With a renewed sense of determination, Shastry mounted the bike again and continued the journey, the road ahead still long but now filled with purpose.

By the time 9:00 a.m. rolled around, Shastry had reached Bijapur, his mind abuzz with thoughts of what lay ahead. The case wasn't over—far from it. But the events of the past 24 hours had given him new clarity. This wasn't just about the law now—it was about justice, something deeper than any legal code could describe.

He parked the bike in front of his lodge, the familiar creaking sign swaying in the morning breeze. The lodge owner, a burly man with a kind face, greeted him with a curious look.

"You're back, sir. How was the village?" the owner asked, clearly curious about the village's mystical reputation.

Shastry smiled, a quiet knowing look in his eyes. "It was... different, let's just say that." He paused for a moment before adding, "Can you do me a favor? Book the first VRL bus to Bengaluru for tonight."

The owner nodded, pulling out his phone to make the arrangements. "No problem, sir. You want to leave tonight itself?"

Shastry nodded, already feeling the exhaustion starting to settle in. He was grateful for the Pulsar ride, but the journey had drained him, both physically and mentally. After receiving confirmation that his bus was booked for 7:30 p.m., Shastry thanked the owner and headed up to his room.

The moment Shastry entered his small lodge room, he felt the weight of exhaustion crash over him like a wave. He dropped his bag by the door and collapsed onto the bed, not even bothering to remove his shoes. The soft mattress welcomed him like an old friend, and within moments, Shastry was asleep, his body and mind finally finding rest.

Hours passed in an instant, and by the time he woke up, it was 4:00 p.m. A knock on the door stirred him awake, the room cleaning service reminding him that the day was slipping away.

Shastry groggily got out of bed, his body still sore from the ride. He washed his face with the cold water from the basin, the icy splash waking him up fully. As he gazed at his reflection in the mirror, he couldn't help but feel a sense of transformation. He wasn't the same man who had arrived in Bijapur just days ago. Something had shifted—both in him and in the world around him.

He needed food—real food, something hearty. The Khanaawali down the road didn't disappoint. He ordered a sumptuous vegetarian meal—steaming plates of jolada rotti, palya, anna, sambar, and more. The meal was simple, but it filled him with the warmth and nourishment he needed after such an emotionally and physically taxing journey.

After dinner, Shastry returned to his lodge, refreshed and ready. He packed his belongings methodically, each item reminding him of the journey ahead. By 7:30 p.m., he was ready to board the VRL bus to Bengaluru.

As the bus rumbled down the highway, Shastry slept by the window, staring out at the passing landscape. The darkness outside was comforting, allowing him to reflect without distractions. The cool air-conditioning and the gentle hum of the engine lulled him into a meditative state.

He thought about Paapa, about the witnesses, about the rituals at the Bhagyawanthi temple. He thought about the law—the one he had studied for years—and how it seemed so limited now, so inadequate to handle the complexities of human nature and divine intervention.

There was so much left to do. 15 days—that's all the time he had until the case resumed. Shastry knew that those 15 days would be critical. He needed to plan, to strategize, to prepare for what would come next. But deep down, he also knew that he wasn't alone in this battle.

As the bus sped along the dark highway, Shastry felt the goddess's presence beside him, her voice echoing softly in his mind.

"Bhagyawanthi is with you, Shastry. Always."

And with that, Shastry closed his eyes, a faint smile tugging at his lips. He wasn't just a lawyer anymore. He was a man on a mission, guided by forces beyond the mortal realm. The journey ahead was long, but for the first time in his life, Shastry knew that he was exactly where he was meant to be.

RETURN TO BENGALURU

Shastry had barely stepped foot in Bengaluru when the fever hit him like a train. For two days, he was confined to his small, rented 1BHK apartment, bundled in a blanket, shivering with chills, only dragging himself out of bed to visit the doctor or swallow another dose of bitter medicine.

The apartment was not exactly the place for recovery but it was home—for now. His tiny living room and the corner where his law books lay stacked were cluttered with case files. The Bijapur case haunted him like a ghost, every thought dragging him back to the village, to Bhagyawanthi, and to the faces of Shivappa and Thimmappa.

Shastry begrudgingly made his way to the nearby Dr. Kamath's clinic. The waiting room was crowded, with people coughing and sneezing around him. Shastry slumped into a plastic chair, sweating profusely and clutching his forehead.

When his turn finally came, Dr. Kamath—a strict but kind-hearted man in his 60s, with thick glasses and a habit of speaking rapidly—was already flipping through Shastry's old records as he entered the room.

"Ah, Mr. Shastry, back again, I see!" Dr. Kamath said with a raised eyebrow. "What is it this time? Overwork? Stress? Lack of sleep? And let me guess, cigarettes again, isn't it?"

Shastry, groaning, collapsed into the chair in front of the doctor's desk. "It's just a fever, Doc. Happens to the best of us."

Dr. Kamath wagged a finger at him. "Fever, yes, but it's because your immune system is tired! I've told you before—those cigarettes are killing you!"

Shastry rolled his eyes, knowing what was coming next. "Yes, yes, Doc. No smoking. Got it."

But Dr. Kamath wasn't done. "I'll prescribe some medicine, but more than that, you need to rest! No spicy food, no cigarettes, no stress. You young advocates think you're invincible, but let me tell you, if you don't take care, the only case you'll be handling is your own in the hospital!"

Shastry nodded, half-listening, while his mind drifted to the cigarette box in his pocket. The doctor scribbled down some names on a prescription pad and handed it over.

Shastry made his way to the local pharmacy, a tiny, cramped store with rows of shelves packed with colorful boxes of pills and syrups. The pharmacist, Madesha, was an enthusiastic middle-aged man with a permanent grin and a tendency to over-explain everything.

Shastry handed him the prescription, and Rajesh scanned it with exaggerated concentration.

"Ah, Dr. Kamath's favorite fever medicine, I see. Very good, very good. This one will knock the fever right out of you! And this... well, this one will help your body regain strength. But you see, it's important to take them on time! Fever doesn't wait for you, sir. It just strikes, and these medicines are like soldiers in a war. Timing is key!"

Shastry smirked weakly. "So, how much is the war effort going to cost me, Madesha?"

Rajesh chuckled and quickly added up the price. "Just 450 rupees, sir. You'll be back on your feet in no time! But remember, no smoking with these pills, okay? You don't want the soldiers to be fighting a losing battle, do you?"

With his medicine in hand, Shastry nodded and headed back to his apartment, wondering when this tirade about smoking would end.

Surprisingly, by the third morning, Shastry felt like a new man. The fever had broken overnight, and he woke up at 5:30 a.m., feeling fresh and energetic, a sense of clarity washing over him. It was as if his body had hit the reset button after two days of rest.

"No more Shivappa's case in mind for the next 7 days!" Shastry told himself sternly, pulling on his sneakers for his usual morning jog at the local playground.

The familiar path of the playground, filled with early risers and elderly folks doing their morning walks, brought him a sense of peace. He jogged three laps, breathing in the cool morning air, his mind finally free of the burden that had weighed him down.

Later that morning, after a hot shower and a simple breakfast of idli and coconut chutney, Shastry made his way to the office, determined to leave the Bhagyawanthi case behind for a week. The ceiling still leaked during the monsoons, and the smell of damp paper filled the room, but it was his space—his tiny fortress.

The first order of the day was his usual visit to Ramesh, the friendly shopkeeper. As soon as Shastry approached, Ramesh grinned. "Ah, Shastry saar, back to life! Tea, cigarette, biscuit, and banana—your usual prescription?"

Shastry chuckled. "That's exactly what I need, Ramesh. Make it strong."

As he took a sip of the hot tea, followed by a puff of his cigarette (despite the doctor's warnings), Shastry felt relaxed for the first time in weeks. It was a strange comfort—the smell of the street, the chatter of usual 'Adda Boys' visiting the stall, and the bite of the biscuit between sips of chai.

Feeling reinvigorated, Shastry decided it was time to solve another problem—his bike. His Discover 125cc was good, but it didn't have the power or style of the Pulsar 150cc he had tasted during his journey. He wanted a new bike—something bigger, faster, and more powerful.

His first stop was a bank, where the branch manager, a man with a round face and thinning hair, barely looked up from his papers when Shastry walked in.

"Loan for a Bike, sir? And... you're an advocate?" the manager asked, looking over the rim of his glasses with a mild frown.

"Yes, I'm a practicing lawyer. I just need a small loan for the bike; I'll pay it off within three years."

The manager shook his head. "Advocates are not on the favorable list, sir. High risk! You people don't have regular incomes."

Shastry was dumbfounded. "High risk? We argue your cases in court when you get into trouble, but we're a high risk for a loan? You must be joking!"

The manager shrugged, unconcerned. "Sorry, sir. It's policy. Next, please."

Undeterred, Shastry tried two more banks, but received the same answer. Each manager had the same expression of mild amusement mixed with dismissal, treating him as if being an advocate was some sort of disadvantage. He left each bank more frustrated than the last. "Buggers!" Shastry muttered under his breath after the third rejection.

Finally, his friend Shekhar, another lawyer, suggested the Advocates Co-operative Society.

"They understand our situation, Shastry. Plus, the interest rate is reasonable. Give it a shot," Shekhar said with a grin.

With nothing to lose, Shastry applied. To his surprise, the society processed his application quickly, and within a day, they approved a loan on favorable terms. Shastry couldn't believe his luck. The down-payment was minimal, and after selling off his Discover 125cc, he was finally able to buy the bike he had been dreaming of—a brand new black Pulsar 150cc.

For the next few days, Shastry focused on everything except the Bijapur case. He relished the feeling of riding his Pulsar around Bengaluru, zipping through the city streets, stopping at tea stalls, and chatting with fellow advocates. The pressures of the past few weeks felt distant, almost like another lifetime. But somewhere in the back of his mind, the case lingered, waiting to resurface.

By the end of the week, Shastry knew it was time to face reality again. But for now, he was ready. The Pulsar hummed beneath him, and with a newfound energy, Shastry knew he had the strength to take on whatever lay ahead. The battle was far from over, but Shastry was ready for it.

THE TRIAL ULTIMATE

The air was cool as Shastry boarded the VRL sleeper bus to Bijapur, his mind already racing with the events that lay ahead. The hearing for S.C. No. 143/2009 was less than 24 hours away, and Shastry had done everything in his power to prepare. But there was something strange about this case; the rituals, and Bhagyawanthi's decree all swirled in his mind like a storm he couldn't control. Despite the strangeness of it all, he knew that the next day would be a turning point.

After settling into his bunk, he pulled out his phone and browsed through his notes one last time. But as the rhythmic hum of the bus lulled him into a state of calm, he put the phone away and closed his eyes, letting the motion of the road and the soft drone of the engine carry him into a restless sleep.

By the time Shastry stepped off the bus in Bijapur, the city was just waking up. The streets were alive with vendors setting up stalls, schoolchildren hurrying past, and the usual clatter of morning activity. Shastry, went to his usual lodge and checked in. Without wasting any time, he freshened up and headed for a quick, local breakfast—a steaming plate of Girmit, a crispy Mirchi Bajji, and, of course, a strong cup of tea. The spicy flavors hit him like a jolt of energy, awakening his senses as he took a drag from his cigarette, the smoke curling lazily into the air. After a quick banana to round off the meal, he headed towards the courthouse.

By the time he arrived at the Bijapur District Court, the sun was climbing higher in the sky, casting long shadows across the court complex. S.C. No. 143/2009 was listed as Item No. 34, and Shastry was in the courtroom by 10:30 a.m., fully prepared for what was to come.

As Shastry stepped into the court hall, he was met by the familiar clamor of advocates rushing around with their files, clerks whispering to their seniors, and the low murmur of litigants waiting anxiously for their cases to be called. But this time, there was a different tension in the air. Everyone seemed to know that the case of Shivappa and Thimmappa had taken on a life of its own.

Outside, Shivappa and Thimmappa stood in handcuffs, flanked by policemen. They wore the same grim expressions they always did, but there was something else in their eyes today—a quiet confidence, as if they knew something the others didn't.

Kalappa, the investigating officer, wasn't taking any chances this time. He had arrived with 15 police personnel, all standing on high alert, keeping a watchful eye on the 38 villagers who had been summoned as witnesses. Kalappa still hadn't forgotten the chaos from the last hearing, and he was determined to avoid a repeat performance.

Inside the courtroom, Public Prosecutor Mammani sat at the front, flipping through his notes with a distracted air. He was unaware of the events that had transpired in the village over the last few days, but he had a sinking feeling in his gut—the case was slipping away. The weight of it pressed down on him, though he couldn't quite pinpoint why. The tension in the courtroom was palpable, thick enough to cut with a knife. Every corner of the Bijapur District Court buzzed with anticipation, but no one dared to speak above a whisper. Shastry sat at the front of the room, his posture composed, but his mind alert, sharp as a blade. S.C. No. 143/2009, the double murder case of Shivappa and Thimmappa, was about to reach a critical turning point.

By now, Shastry was more than just an advocate. He had become entangled in the village's ancient web of power, secrets, and tradition. The events of the last few days still echoed in his mind: the village, Bhagyawanthi's decree, the 38 witnesses who had been swayed by forces far beyond the courtroom. But today was the day. The witnesses had been brought to testify.

In his seat, Mammani shuffled through his papers, the weight of the case heavy on his shoulders. He could sense something was wrong, a nagging doubt that had taken root ever since the morning began. His case, once so ironclad, was slowly slipping through his fingers. His strategy hinged on the testimonies of these witnesses

At exactly 11:00 a.m., the sharp voice of the court attender rang through the hall.

"Silence!"

The room fell into an immediate hush as Judge Subramanya entered, his face set in its usual mask of calm authority. His black robes fluttered behind him as he took his seat on the bench, his sharp eyes scanning the room.

Without wasting time, he began the day's proceedings, going through the cases on the cause list methodically. The minutes dragged on as case after case was addressed, but the tension in the room kept mounting, like a rope being pulled tighter and tighter.

Finally, the moment arrived. The court clerk called out:

"S.C. No. 143/2009!"

Shastry rose to his feet and approached the podium, as did Mammani. The two men exchanged brief nods, but the air between them was charged. Kalappa, standing at the back, motioned to the constables, who immediately brought Shivappa and Thimmappa into the courtroom.

The judge's eyes flicked to Kalappa. "Are the witnesses present?"

Kalappa, standing stiffly at attention, nodded. "Yes, Your Honor. All 38 witnesses are here."

Judge Subramanya eyed the long line of villagers seated at the back, then turned back to his docket. "Very well. Let's proceed."

By 12:30 p.m., the courtroom had settled once again, and the clerk called out the case for the second time. The tension in the room was palpable as PW1 was called to the stand—Veeraiah, a frail, middle-aged man with hands calloused from years of farm labor.

"Call PW1 to the stand. Veeraiah," the court clerk announced, his voice echoing through the room.

A frail man in his mid-40s, Veeraiah, slowly made his way to the witness box. His steps were hesitant, as if the weight of his decision bore down on him with every step. His clothes, worn and faded from years of hard labor in the fields, hung loosely on his thin frame. He glanced nervously around the courtroom, avoiding eye contact with both Mammani and the judge. Veeraiah was sworn in, and Mammani wasted no time in launching into his questioning. "Veeraiah, tell the court what happened on the day of the murders," Mammani said, his voice firm but controlled. Veeraiah looked down at his hands, his fingers twitching nervously. When he finally spoke, his voice was barely above a whisper.

"Sahebre, I don't know anything."

The courtroom fell silent. Mammani froze, not quite believing what he had just heard. He leaned forward, his eyes narrowing.

"What do you mean, you don't know anything? You were present on the day of the incident, were you not?"

Veeraiah shifted uncomfortably, his gaze still fixed on his hands. "The police brought me here today. They asked me to put my thumb impression on some papers. I didn't know what they were for. I'm illiterate, sahebre."

Mammani's jaw tightened. Hostile witness!

Judge Subramanya made a note on his order sheet and spoke in his usual calm, authoritative voice. "PW1 has turned hostile. Call the next witness."

Next up was PW2 Jagganna, a stocky, middle-aged farmer with a bushy mustache and hands rough from years of tilling the soil. As he approached the witness stand, he too avoided looking at anyone in the room, his shoulders hunched in unease. After taking the oath, Mammani, trying to regain his composure, began again.

"Jagganna, you were present on the day of the incident. Can you please tell the court what you witnessed?"

Jagganna cleared his throat nervously and, in a voice barely louder than a murmur, replied, "Sahebre, I don't know anything."

Mammani blinked, clearly growing frustrated. "Nothing? You were present in the village when the murders happened, weren't you?"

"No, sahebre. The police asked me to come today. I didn't see anything. I wasn't there."

The courtroom stirred slightly. Two witnesses in a row had turned hostile. Mammani's case was crumbling before his eyes, and he knew it. But he pressed on.

When PW3 Boraiah was called, the courtroom was already buzzing with whispers. Boraiah, a tall, lanky man with deep-set eyes, stepped into the witness box with the same hesitance as the others. He fidgeted with his fingers, clearly uncomfortable being there.

Mammani's voice carried an edge of desperation now. "Boraiah, what did you see on the day of the murders? Were you there?"

Boraiah avoided Mammani's gaze, looking down at the floor as he answered, "Sahebre, I didn't see anything. The police asked me to come. I don't know what happened."

By this point, Judge Subramanya was clearly growing frustrated. He made another note on the order sheet before looking up at Mammani.

"PW3 has also turned hostile. Call the next witness," the judge said, his voice tight with impatience.

Shankra, a heavyset man with a round face and nervous eyes, was next. He shifted his weight uncomfortably as he stood before the judge. Mammani, now visibly frustrated, began the examination. "Shankra, tell the court what you know about the events of that day. You were there. What did you see?"

Shankra shook his head quickly. "I don't know anything, sahebre. The police told me to come. I didn't see anything."

The pattern continued with PW5 Bajappa, a burly man in his 50s. His testimony was almost identical to the others. "I wasn't there, sahebre. The police told me to put my thumbprint on something. I don't know what it was for," Bajappa mumbled, shifting from foot to foot as he spoke.

Mammani's shoulders sagged with defeat. Five witnesses had now turned hostile, and he could feel the case slipping away from him entirely.

By the time PW6 Mankanna was called, the mood in the courtroom had shifted. Everyone could sense that the case was falling apart. Mankanna, a thin, wiry man with a nervous disposition, took the stand and, like the others, claimed ignorance.

"I don't know anything. I didn't see anything," Mankanna said quickly, as though eager to leave the witness box as soon as possible.

Parimala, one of the few female witnesses, approached the stand with her head bowed, her hands clutching the ends of her saree tightly. When Mammani asked her what she had seen, her response was the same as the others.

"I wasn't there, sahebre. I don't know anything."

PW8 Dasaiah, a wiry man with a grizzled beard, gave an identical response. "I wasn't there. The police told me to come, but I don't know what happened."

The next witness, PW9 Naganna, was no different. "Sahebre, I wasn't there. I don't know anything."

As PW10 Basava took the stand, the courtroom had descended into complete disbelief. Witness after witness had turned hostile, and Basava's testimony was no different. "I didn't see anything, sahebre. I don't know what happened."

Radhamma, the final witness examined and she, approached the stand with a steely expression. She took the oath, but her response was the same. "I don't know anything. I wasn't there. The police brought me here."

By the time PW11's testimony was completed, Mammani looked like a man who had been beaten into submission. His carefully prepared case had crumbled before his eyes, and there was nothing left for him to salvage. Each witness had turned hostile, repeating the same story: they knew nothing, they had seen nothing.

Judge Subramanya leaned back in his chair, his fingers tapping lightly on the desk.

"Mr. Mammani," he said slowly, "There is no use in wasting the court's time. You've now presented eleven witnesses, and not a single one has given a testimony worth considering." The silence in the courtroom was deafening. Mammani's face flushed with embarrassment as the judge continued.

"I'll call this case after lunch. If you have sterling witnesses, bring them onto the box or else better give up your evidence."

Mammani could only nod, his voice caught in his throat as he packed up his files. His mind raced as he walked back to his chambers, knowing full well that there was no witness left who would testify in favor of the prosecution.

As the courtroom emptied for lunch, Shastry sat back in his chair, watching the 38 witnesses shuffle out of the room, their eyes averted from everyone else. Bhagyawanthi's decree echoed in his mind, and a quiet satisfaction settled over him. The witnesses had been silenced—but not by him.

Shastry walked out into the sunlit courtyard, as he reflected on the morning's events. The case wasn't over yet, but Shastry knew that the battle had already been won.

The courtroom buzzed with tension as Judge Subramanya rose for the lunch recess, the air thick with anticipation. Mammani sat at his desk, surrounded by the wreckage of his case, as witness after witness had turned hostile that morning. His mind raced. Eleven witnesses—all of them had crumbled, refusing to testify, each one giving him nothing but blank stares and rehearsed denials. What had happened?

As the villagers exited the courtroom in a quiet, orderly fashion, Mammani saw his last hope slip through his fingers. The case he had built, piece by piece, was falling apart. Desperate, he decided to take one last shot. He followed the villagers into the court's yard, pleading with them, his voice rising in panic.

"Please, you must testify! You know the truth—you were there! If you don't speak, justice will not be served!" he urged, his words spilling out like a man who had lost all sense of decorum.

But the villagers stood in silence. Their faces were blank, their expressions unreadable, as though they were staring through him, beyond him, beyond the court itself. Their eyes reflected a certain transcendental calm, a kind of stillness that terrified Mammani more than any words could have.

They had made their decision—Bhagyawanthi's decree had been fulfilled. There would be no more testimony.

With a heavy heart and the bitter taste of defeat on his lips, Mammani knew it was over.

Shastry, on the other hand, was anything but concerned. The courtroom's heavy air had followed him out the doors and dissipated into the warm Bijapur afternoon, where life went on as usual, unaffected by the courtroom drama.

Shastry strolled to a small, roadside hotel just outside the court complex—the kind of place he loved. The food here was simple but delicious, and after the grueling morning session, he was craving a good meal.

He ordered his usual: a steaming plate of jolada rotti, served with spicy brinjal curry and a side of chutney. The tangy flavors exploded in his mouth as he took his first bite, the heat from the curry making him break into a slight sweat. This is what life was about, he thought, smiling to himself. Food, work, and a cigarette to top it off.

Once his meal was done, he stepped outside the hotel, lit a cigarette, and took a long drag, letting the smoke drift up into the sky. He stood there, his thoughts momentarily far away from the court, savoring the coolness of the breeze and the satisfaction of the meal. With the trial winding down, there was little left for him to do but see the endgame through.

After finishing his cigarette, Shastry walked over to beeda stall and indulged himself on a saada beeda, its fragrant spices and fresh leaves calling to him. He popped the sweet concoction into his mouth, chewing slowly as he made his way back to the court.

By the time Shastry returned to the courtroom, Judge Subramanya had already taken his seat, his face showing its usual calm. The courtroom was full once again—lawyers shuffled papers, clerks whispered to each other, and the constables lined up Shivappa and Thimmappa in their usual place.

At 2:00 p.m., the tension returned as the clerk announced, "S.C. No. 143/2009"

The judge immediately turned to Mammani, his voice sharp and authoritative. "Mr. Mammani, have you been able to secure any witnesses for testimony? What is your decision regarding the case?"

Mammani stood slowly, his body weighed down with defeat. "Your Honor, after speaking to the witnesses during the recess, I regret to inform you that I was unable to secure the testimony of any of the remaining witnesses. I... I intend to give up my side of evidence."

The admission hung in the air like a death knell for the prosecution. Judge Subramanya nodded, his face betraying no emotion. This case was unraveling faster than anyone could have anticipated.

"Very well," the judge said, his voice steady. "In light of the prosecution's inability to produce any further evidence, I will now proceed with recording the statements of the accused under Section 313 of the Cr.P.C."

Shastry turned to Shivappa and Thimmappa, his face calm but his mind focused. He had prepared them well for this moment, and they both knew exactly what to say.

Shivappa was the first to approach the dock, his hands in a folded position. He was sworn in, and the judge looked him directly in the eye.

"Shivappa, do you wish to make a statement regarding the charges against you?"

Shivappa, maintaining the same composure he had shown throughout the trial, replied, "Sahebre, I am innocent. I have not committed any crime. These charges against me are false. I did not kill Mohan or Beerappa. I am not guilty."

The same process was repeated for Thimmappa, who echoed his brother's words with the same level of conviction.

"I have not committed any crime, sahebre. I am innocent of these accusations."

With the statements recorded, Judge Subramanya turned to Shastry. His gaze was steady, but there was an undercurrent of expectation in his tone.

"Mr. Shastry, do you have anything to argue?"

Shastry rose from his seat and walked to the podium, his heart pounding but his mind focused. He had rehearsed this moment many times in his head, and now it was time to deliver the final blow. The courtroom fell silent as everyone waited for Shastry's words.

"Your Honor," Shastry began, his voice calm but commanding, "the prosecution has, from the very beginning, failed to establish a prima facie case against my clients. Today, we have seen eleven witnesses—key witnesses—who were supposedly present on the day of the murders. And yet, not a single one has testified in favor of the prosecution's version of events. Not one."

He paused, letting the weight of his words settle over the room.

"The police have relied solely on thumbprints from illiterate villagers who have been coerced into signing papers they cannot read. Not one piece of credible evidence has been presented to this court to prove that my clients, Shivappa and Thimmappa, were involved in this heinous crime. No motive has been proven, and no weapon has been recovered that links them to the murders."

Shastry glanced at Mammani, whose face was pale with resignation.

"Your Honor, in the absence of any evidence—no confessions, no credible witness testimony, no material objects connecting my clients to the crime—I submit that there is no case left to be made by the prosecution. The only conclusion that can be drawn is that my clients are innocent."

He stepped back from the podium, his final words hanging in the air like a sharp-edged blade.

Judge Subramanya leaned back in his chair, his sharp mind sifting through the facts. He had seen cases like this before—cases where the evidence was shaky, the witnesses unreliable, and the prosecution grasping at straws. But this case was unique. The prosecution's side had collapsed, leaving nothing but rumors and circumstantial evidence.

He glanced at Shivappa and Thimmappa, two men who had sat through the trial with a calmness that intrigued him. Their villagers had turned their backs on the prosecution, and the defense's argument was unassailable. The law was clear—no evidence, no conviction.

With a slight nod to the stenographer, the judge began to dictate his judgment.

"In the matter of S.C. No. 143/2009, the prosecution has failed to present any credible evidence to substantiate the charges of murder against the accused, Shivappa and Thimmappa. The witnesses presented have turned hostile, and there has been no material evidence submitted to link the accused to the crime."

"In light of these facts, the court finds that the prosecution has not proved its case beyond reasonable doubt. I hereby acquit the accused, Shivappa and Thimmappa, of all charges."

A murmur rippled through the courtroom, but Judge Subramanya remained composed as he finished his dictation. He looked up from his papers and spoke, his voice clear.

"(Bidugade Aagide!!) You are free to go."

Shastry and Mammani rose up together and bowed down before the Court. Shivappa and Thimmappa also followed the suit.

The air outside the courthouse was crisp and filled with murmurs of the recently concluded trial. The sun hung low in the sky, casting long shadows across the Bijapur District Court, as Shivappa and Thimmappa stepped outside, now free men. Their eyes, wide with disbelief and joy, searched for Shastry, who was walking behind them, deep in thought.

The two brothers turned and rushed toward him, their faces brimming with gratitude. Shivappa, the older of the two, clasped Shastry's hands with reverence, his voice quivering with emotion.

"Sahebre, you have saved our lives! You are not just a lawyer to us—you have been sent by Bhagyawanthi herself. It was her will, and you, who made this happen! How can we ever repay you?" Shivappa's voice cracked as he spoke, his eyes glistening with tears.

Thimmappa, standing beside his brother, nodded solemnly, unable to find words. They believed with every fiber of their being that Shastry had been chosen by the deity to guide them through this storm. To them, Shastry wasn't just a lawyer—he was a divine intervention, a symbol of hope.

Shastry, for all his logical reasoning and legal acumen, felt the weight of their belief. He was no stranger to the intersection of faith and law, having witnessed it throughout his career. But today, their devotion to Bhagyawanthi and their unwavering trust in him left him humbled.

"You don't owe me anything, Shivappa, Thimmappa." Shastry smiled softly, placing a reassuring hand on each of their shoulders. "You both had truth on your side. The rest was Bhagyawanthi's will, and maybe, just maybe, I was meant to play a part. Go back to your village, live your lives peacefully, and remember, the law doesn't always give answers, but truth finds its way."

The brothers, still emotional, folded their hands and bowed deeply to Shastry, then turned and walked away, heading back to their village with their hearts light and their future restored.

Shastry watched them disappear into the crowd, their silhouettes fading as they returned to their lives. For him, though, the day wasn't quite over. The weight of the trial, the extraordinary circumstances, and the interplay between law and belief lingered in his mind like a fog he couldn't shake.

He made his way back to his lodge, feeling the need to reflect. With a couple of hours to kill before his bus back to Bengaluru, he indulged himself in a familiar ritual—Old Monk rum mixed with Thums Up. It was his go-to when he wanted to unwind, especially after a long day in court. He climbed the narrow stairs to the terrace of the lodge, a peaceful spot where he could be alone with his thoughts.

On the terrace, the breeze was cool, carrying the scent of freshly bloomed flowers and distant cooking fires. He opened his bottle, poured a generous amount of Old Monk into his tumbler, and topped it with Thums Up. He took a deep drag from his cigarette, the smoke curling lazily into the evening sky. The world felt far away, distant, as he sat there with his drink, watching the last vestiges of sunlight sink behind the hills.

He had brought along a small packet of savories from a nearby shop—crispy, spicy snacks that paired well with his drink. As he chewed, his mind wandered, unraveling the events of the past few weeks.

"Who were Shivappa and Thimmappa?" he thought, taking another sip. Two brothers, caught in a web of fate, dragged into the harshness of the law. And who was Shastry in all of this? Was he simply a lawyer, or had he been pulled into this case by forces beyond his control? The villagers' belief in Bhagyawanthi was so strong, so deeply ingrained in their culture, that it almost seemed as if the divine will had truly influenced the outcome.

Shastry chuckled softly to himself, exhaling a long breath of cigarette smoke. He wasn't the superstitious type, but the case had made him question the very foundations of justice, law, and belief.

His mind turned to criminal jurisprudence, the principles he had studied so meticulously in law school. Actus Reus—the physical act of committing a crime. Mens Rea—the intent, the guilty mind. And then there was reasonable doubt. Where did all those principles go? Shastry wondered. He had built his case around these pillars of law, yet, standing in that courtroom, watching witness after witness turn hostile, none of it seemed to matter.

In the end, it wasn't Actus Reus or Mens Rea that won the day. It was Bhagyawanthi's decree, whispered through the mouths of the villagers, silently conveyed in their refusal to testify. Where did the law end and faith begin? Shastry couldn't tell anymore. The two had intertwined in a way that left him unsettled.

He sipped his drink, letting the warmth of the rum spread through him, grounding him in the moment. India, he mused, was a land of rich traditions, ancient cultures, and deep spirituality. Here, the law wasn't just about statutes and precedents; it was about understanding the souls of the people, their history, their customs and their Gods.

"There's so much more to learn," Shastry whispered to himself, staring at the darkening horizon. He realized that despite his legal knowledge, despite the courtrooms he had entered, he had to still learn. Learning Law was not enough. He still had to Learn Life.

The clock ticked on, and soon it was time for Shastry to pack his things and head to the bus stand. He boarded the VRL bus, settling into his seat by the window, watching as the bus pulled away from Bijapur and began its journey back to Bengaluru. The hum of the engine, the gentle rocking of the bus, soothed him.

As the familiar sights of Bijapur slipped away, Shastry felt a profound sense of peace. The case had taken him to places he never thought he'd go, both physically and mentally. But now, as the bus carried him back home, he felt lighter. The case of S.C. No. 143/2009 was behind him, and with it, a deeper understanding of his path as a lawyer, and more importantly, as a man.

The rumble of the bus, the cool night air, and the memories of the past few weeks washed over him as he leaned back in his seat, closing his eyes.

In his mind, he could still hear the distant, calming voice of Bhagyawanthi, guiding him forward, reminding him that the journey was far from over. UNTILL NEXT TIME!!

Chapter - II
BEYOND THE KNOWN

2011- FEBRUARY OF CHANGE

The morning sun cast a dim glow over the crumbling streets of Bengaluru, the air thick with the hum of early traffic and the distant murmur of street vendors setting up for the day. In a small, worn-down house tucked away in the slums of Srirampura, Padma sat on the floor, scrubbing dishes with a kind of quiet determination. Her hands moved quickly, but her mind was elsewhere—on her son, Mahesh, and the storm that had engulfed their lives.

For Padma, life had always been a battle. Working as a maid in others' homes, she cleaned dishes, wiped floors, and washed clothes, earning just enough to scrape by. Her husband had abandoned her long ago, leaving her with Mahesh, a child born out of an illicit affair that had left scars deeper than any financial struggle. The man still supported them, but only in name, with a few rupees tossed their way each month—barely enough to keep the lights on. And his love? That was something neither Padma nor Mahesh had ever felt.

Mahesh, now 19, was at a crossroads. He had recently completed his 12th standard at a government college, but graduation and Degree College seemed like a distant dream. His mother had been pushing him to continue his education, to pursue a degree and change the course of their lives. But Mahesh, in his heart, felt that the time for school was over. His mother worked tirelessly, and seeing her come home with aching bones and worn hands gnawed at him daily. He felt it was his duty now to step up, to help her, to take on the burden she carried.

That afternoon, Mahesh had gone out with his friends, his mind swirling with indecision and frustration. He knew what his mother wanted, but he couldn't shake the feeling that he had to do more—something immediate, something that would ease her suffering now, not years from now.

While he was out, the storm hit. The landlord, Prakash Gowda, a man known for his temper and ruthless nature, arrived at their home, his voice booming as he demanded six months of overdue rent. Padma, standing frail in her small house, tried to reason with him, her voice shaking as she promised to pay soon. But Prakash was having none of it.

"Do you think I run a charity here?" Prakash shouted, his face red with rage. "Six months, Padma! Six months you haven't paid a single paisa! You think you can live here for free?"

Padma begged him to give her just a few more days, but the man's temper flared. He stormed into the house, pulling down shelves, throwing their belongings outside, creating a scene for all the neighbors to witness. He grabbed Padma by the hair, yanking her to the ground, his voice dripping with venom.

"You think your sob stories will keep me at bay? If you can't pay, then leave! No one cares about your pitiful life!"

The neighbors, helpless, watched in horror as Prakash assaulted Padma, tearing her blouse and throwing her down as if she were nothing. Tears streamed down her face, her sobs echoing through the narrow streets as Prakash finally stormed away, leaving her with the wreckage of their belongings scattered on the road.

Mahesh's phone rang just as he was walking with his friends, trying to find work. A neighbor called, her voice filled with urgency. "Mahesh, come home! Your mother—Prakash Gowda—he's... just come home, quick!"

Mahesh's heart sank as he rushed back, his mind racing with fear and rage. When he arrived, the sight that greeted him made his blood boil. His mother, still trembling, was picking up their scattered belongings, her torn saree barely covering her as she sobbed quietly. Mahesh's hands clenched into fists, his rage building like a storm inside him. He had never felt this kind of fury before, but the sight of his mother, broken and humiliated, ignited something dark within him. He swore revenge. He would make Prakash Gowda pay, even if it cost him everything.

In the following days, Mahesh struggled to find a job, driven by a singular desire—to save his mother from this life. But no job came. He knocked on doors, filled out applications, but everywhere he went, he was turned away. His frustration grew, and so did his desperation. That was when he met them—a group of local boys, rough around the edges, known troublemakers. They saw the anger in Mahesh, the fire that flickered in his eyes, and they knew they could use it. "You want to make money?" one of them asked, flashing a dangerous grin. "We can help you. Join us. We're with Contractor Krishna. He runs things around here."

Contractor Krishna was a name whispered with both fear and respect in the underbelly of North Bengaluru. He controlled the streets, his hands in everything—from extortion to petty theft, from raiding pubs to terrorizing shopkeepers. And now, Mahesh was about to step into this world.

The day Mahesh was introduced to Contractor Krishna, he felt a mix of fear and excitement. Krishna, a burly man with a wild, intimidating presence, looked Mahesh up and down, his eyes gleaming with approval. "So, this is the new recruit?" Krishna said with a grin that made Mahesh's stomach churn. "Good. We need someone with fire. You're just in time, too. We've got a little job to do."

Krishna handed Mahesh a hockey stick, his fingers lingering on the weapon for just a moment before letting it go. "You'll ride with us tonight, kid. Let's see if you've got what it takes."

They piled into a Maruti van, the gang of six squeezing inside, their energy electric as they headed toward their target—a small jewelry shop run by Chandu Lal. Mahesh was riding pillion on a bike which followed, the wind rushing past his face as the city's narrow streets blurred into a mix of lights and shadows. When they arrived, Krishna led the charge, storming into the shop with the others trailing behind. They demanded Rs.2,00,000.00 their voices loud and commanding. When Chandu Lal refused, Krishna's smile vanished, replaced by something far more sinister.

With a swift, brutal swing, Krishna struck Chandu Lal with his wooden club, the crack of bone against wood echoing through the shop. Mahesh stood frozen, clutching the hockey stick, his heart pounding in his ears as Krishna attacked Lal with a ferocity that left him crumpled and bleeding. The gang didn't steal a rupee. They left in a hurry, fearing that Lal was dead.

Mahesh felt sick. His hands trembled as they sped away, the siren of approaching police cars ringing in the distance. He had joined the gang for money, for survival, but now he was in the deep end of underworld.

The air inside the Maruti van was thick with silence as the gang sped back to their hideout, the tension from the brutal attack on Chandu Lal still buzzing like electricity. Mahesh sat in the pillion seat of the bike, gripping the hockey stick tightly, his heart pounding in his chest. His mind swirled with a strange mix of adrenaline and fear, the events of the past few moments playing on a loop in his head. He had crossed a line—he knew it. But what haunted him more was the question why he didn't feel guilty.

As they turned into a narrow alley, the van following closely behind, Mahesh's eyes caught a familiar figure. There, standing by a small condiments shop, was Prakash Gowda, sipping tea casually, a cigarette dangling from his lips. The sight of the man who had humiliated his mother just days ago made Mahesh's blood boil. The rage he thought had subsided resurfaced with violent intensity.

His grip tightened on the hockey stick.

"Stop the bike!" Mahesh shouted suddenly, his voice sharp with anger.

The bike screeched to a halt, and the Maruti van following behind jerked to a stop as well. Krishna, who was in the front seat of the van, leaned forward, confused. "What the hell is going on?" he muttered, looking around.

Without another word, Mahesh jumped off the bike, his eyes locked on Prakash Gowda, who was still obliviously enjoying his tea. The fire inside Mahesh roared to life, and he felt his feet moving faster than his thoughts.

"Mahesh, what are you doing?!" shouted Kothi, the rider of the bike, but it was too late. Mahesh had already stormed across the street, his hockey stick raised high. Mahesh's breath came in short, sharp bursts as he closed the distance between himself and Prakash Gowda. The world around him seemed to slow down—the clinking of teacups, the distant honking of vehicles, the idle chatter of passersby—all of it faded into a dull hum. His focus narrowed, and the only thing he could see was Prakash.

"Ley Prakasha!" Mahesh yelled, his voice cutting through the air like a knife.

Prakash barely had time to turn around before the hockey stick came crashing down, smashing the teacup out of his hand and sending shards flying. The cigarette fell from his lips as he stumbled backward, shock and confusion washing over his face.

"What the hell?!" Prakash shouted, scrambling to regain his balance, but Mahesh was already on him.

With another swing, Mahesh slammed the hockey stick into Prakash's side, knocking the wind out of him. The crowd around the small shop gasped, some stepping back in shock while others instinctively pulled out their phones to record the chaos.

"You think you can treat my mother like that? Huh?!" Mahesh roared, his voice trembling with rage as he brought the stick down again, this time connecting with Prakash's shoulder. "You think you can just throw her on the ground and get away with it?!"

Prakash, now on his knees, cowered beneath the blows, trying in vain to shield himself with his arms. His voice was hoarse, filled with pain and fear. "Stop! Stop! I didn't mean—"

"Shut up!" Mahesh screamed, his fury blinding him to anything else. With one final, vicious swing, he struck Prakash square in the chest, sending him sprawling to the ground, gasping for breath.

Back at the van, Krishna and the others watched in stunned silence. Even Contractor Krishna, the notorious gangster who had seen his fair share of violence, looked momentarily taken aback by the ferocity of Mahesh's attack. For a moment, no one moved.

"What the hell's he doing?!" Krishna muttered, eyes wide as he leaned forward in his seat, watching the scene unfold.

"He's losing it, guru," Seena, still on the bike, said nervously. He had seen Mahesh angry before, but this was different. This was something darker.

One of the gang members in the back seat, Mohan, leaned out the window, grinning as if the chaos was entertainment. "That's it, Mahesh! Show him who's *Anna Bond*! Finish him off!" he shouted, laughing.

"Yeah! Make him eat his chappal!" another voice joined in from the back, the gang feeding off each other's excitement. Their cheers echoed across the street as Mahesh continued his assault.

But Krishna, while amused, also saw the danger. "Enough, Mahesh, stop!" he yelled, his voice more commanding this time. But Mahesh was beyond hearing.

Prakash, now bleeding from his nose and mouth, lay on the ground, clutching his side in agony. His shirt was torn, and he struggled to breathe, his hands trembling as he tried to push himself up.

Mahesh, panting heavily, stood over him, his eyes burning with hatred. But he wasn't done yet. Not nearly. Without warning, Mahesh dropped the hockey stick, reached down, and grabbed Prakash by the collar, dragging him to his feet.

"You humiliated my mother. You'll pay for that today." Mahesh's voice was low, almost a growl.

With a swift tug, Mahesh tore Prakash's shirt, ripping it clean off and leaving him bare-chested in front of the growing crowd. Prakash, weak and disoriented, tried to cover himself, but Mahesh wasn't done. He grabbed at

Prakash's pants, pulling them down in one brutal motion, leaving the man naked from the waist down.

The crowd gasped in shock, some turning away in embarrassment, while others couldn't help but stare. Prakash's face burned with shame, his once commanding presence reduced to a whimpering, naked man in the middle of the street.

Mahesh stood back, breathing heavily, his fists clenched, as he watched Prakash struggle to his feet.

"Run, you bastard! Run like the dog you are!" Mahesh shouted, his voice filled with disgust.

And Prakash, with nothing left to lose, stumbled to his feet and did just that—he ran, naked, down the main road, his shame on full display for everyone to see.

Back at the van, Krishna watched with a mix of amusement and admiration. He leaned back in his seat, chuckling darkly.

"Well, damn. Didn't think the kid had it in him," Krishna said, a crooked grin spreading across his face. "Didn't need to strip the guy, but hell, I like his style."

The gang laughed along with him, the initial shock fading into a shared sense of thrill. For them, this was just another day—violence and intimidation were their bread and butter. But for Mahesh, it was a turning point, a moment he could never take back.

"Let's get out of here before the cops show up," Krishna finally said, nodding to the driver. "Kid's earned his spot with us. He's one of us now."

Mahesh, breathing hard and still fuming, climbed back onto the bike. His heart was still racing, but something inside him had settled—the thirst for revenge had been momentarily quenched.

As they drove away from the scene, Mahesh's eyes remained locked on the shrinking figure of Prakash Gowda, running naked down the street, his dignity shattered. This was only the beginning, Mahesh thought. He had entered a world where violence was the answer, and he wasn't sure if he could ever go back.

AT THE POLICE STATION

The police station buzzed with activity, the dull hum of routine paperwork suddenly shattered by the piercing ring of multiple phones going off at once. Inspector Sridhar, a hardened officer known for his no-nonsense approach, was at his desk when the wireless phone crackled to life.

"Sir, there's been an attack at a small jeweler's shop in Bandireddy Street. It's Contractor Krishna's gang."

Sridhar's sharp eyes flicked up; instantly alert. He had been tracking them for months, waiting for the right moment to strike. And today, it seemed, the moment had come.

"Any arrests?" Sridhar asked, his voice crisp and commanding.

"Not yet, sir. But we've got clear information. Krishna and his boys hit a jeweler today, badly injured him. They're holed up in an under-construction building down by the railway track, drinking and celebrating."

Sridhar leaned back in his chair, tapping his pen thoughtfully against the desk. His mind raced through the details—Krishna's gang had been a thorn in his backside for too long. They were getting more brazen, more reckless.

"There's something else, sir," the voice on the other end continued. "Prakash Gowda—a local landlord—he was attacked too. Condiments shop owner says it was a young boy, new to the gang. No complaint from Prakash, though."

Sridhar's brow furrowed. No complaint? That was odd. Prakash should not be the kind of man to let an attack go unnoticed. Something wasn't adding up. There was a new recruit involved. That piqued his interest.

"Alright. Let's move, boys," Sridhar said, standing up abruptly. He grabbed his cap and motioned to his team, who were already on their feet. "Get your gear. We're conducting an operation tonight."

Meanwhile, in an abandoned building on the far-end of Srirampura near the railway track, Krishna's gang was in full swing. The dim glow of lanterns flickered through the construction site as the men sat on overturned crates, bottles of liquor in hand, laughter and crude jokes filling the empty rooms.

Krishna, red-eyed and swaying slightly from the alcohol, leaned back against a half-finished wall, grinning like a king surveying his kingdom. Mahesh sat nearby, quieter than the rest, but his adrenaline from the day's events still coursed through his veins. He was trying to process what had happened—the attack on Chandu Lal, his violent outburst against Prakash Gowda—but the gang's laughter and the haze of smoke made it hard to think clearly.

Krishna raised his bottle, slurring slightly, "Mahesh, my boy! You did well today, Real good. Never seen someone go at it like you did. You've got fire."

The others cheered, clinking their bottles, and Mahesh felt a mix of pride and discomfort. Was this really the life he wanted?

"But now..." Krishna hiccupped, pulling out a crumpled 1000-rupee note from his pocket, "Feed the wolves. Go get us some biryani, kebabs, and don't forget the smokes!"

Mahesh took the money, knowing there was no refusing Krishna in this state. He nodded silently, grabbing his jacket and heading for the door.

Just as Mahesh sped off on the bike, weaving through the narrow streets, Sridhar's police convoy arrived at the under-construction building, headlights cutting through the night. The building was eerily silent, except for the faint sounds of the gang's merrymaking inside.

Sridhar motioned to his team, silent but precise. His heart pounded with anticipation—they had one chance to take these men down.

"Go, go, go!" Sridhar whispered, and in a well-coordinated move, the police officers stormed the building.

Inside, the gang's celebration was abruptly cut short by the sound of footsteps and shouting. For a split second, there was complete silence—then panic erupted.

"It's the cops! Run!" one of the men yelled, stumbling to his feet.

But it was too late. Sridhar's team had already surrounded them. Within seconds, the gang members were pinned to the ground, some trying to resist, others too drunk to make sense of what was happening. Krishna, his drunken bravado slipping away, raised his hands in surrender, his bottle clattering to the floor with sound of the rattling of the wheels of the passing train, playing in the background. The police had caught them off-guard, and there was no escaping this time.

The handcuffs clicked into place, and one by one, the gang members were led out to the waiting police van, their defeat palpable in the cool night air.

As Mahesh rode through the city streets, oblivious to what was unfolding behind him, he felt a strange unease settle over him. Something didn't feel right, though he couldn't put his finger on it.

By the time he returned to the building, the sight that greeted him made his heart drop. Police vans lined the street, their flashing lights illuminating the area. Officers moved in and out of the building, and from where he stood, Mahesh could see Krishna and the others being loaded into the vans, handcuffed and defeated.

Mahesh's instincts kicked in, and without thinking, he slammed on the brakes, the bike coming to a stop just in time. He couldn't be seen here. He couldn't afford to be caught.

His breath quickened, and he knew he had only one option—run. He turned the bike around and sped off into the darkness, the sounds of the city swallowing him whole.

Back at the police station, Inspector Sridhar stood with his arms crossed, surveying the gang members who had been arrested. The room was filled with the clinking of chains and murmurs of conversation between the officers.

Krishna, still in handcuffs, sat on a bench, his face a mask of sullen rage. Sridhar walked over, eyes sharp as ever.

"You thought you could keep running, Krishna? Thought you'd never get caught?" Sridhar's voice was calm but laced with authority. "But where's your new recruit, huh? Where's the kid who made his grand debut today?"

Krishna gave him a sideways glance but said nothing.

"Tell me where the boy is, Krishna." Sridhar's voice dropped, taking on a more dangerous tone. "You and your gang are going down either way, but the boy—he's fresh. He doesn't need to go down the same path as you."

Sridhar frowned. Something about the missing recruit intrigued him. He hadn't expected this—a mystery amidst the chaos.

He called over one of his men. "Get the details on this new kid. We need to know who we're dealing with."

As the officer scrambled to gather more information, Sridhar's mind began to race. Who was this boy? And why hadn't Prakash Gowda filed a complaint after being attacked?

While Inspector Sridhar was contemplating the enigma of the missing recruit, elsewhere, Advocate Ramachandra Shastry was just beginning his day. The sun filtered through the cracks of his small office—once a car shed, now transformed into the modest headquarters of Shastry Law Associates.

Today Shastry's morning ritual involved a cup of strong coffee and a cigarette, with the faint hum of street traffic in the background.

AT SHASTRY LAW ASSOCIATES

The morning was unusually quiet in Shastry's office, the faint hum of traffic outside the only sound interrupting the stillness. Ramachandra Shastry sat at his desk, his sharp eyes scanning the various files piled around him. As he was sipping his coffee, the door creaked open, and a man in his early forties entered with a stiff posture, his face strained with the worries of the world. Pramod Kumar, the manager of a car service station, looked unsure of himself, his hands nervously clutching a set of papers.

"Mr. Shastry?" Pramod began hesitantly. "I've been sent by my friend, your old schoolmate—Supreet. He said you could help with a legal matter."

Shastry gestured for Pramod to take a seat, his expression calm and inviting. "Ah, Supreet! Yes, yes. Sit down. What can I do for you?"

Pramod sank into the chair and cleared his throat. "It's about a boy—Gopala. He's just 21, a driver and mechanic at our service station. Recently, after servicing a car, he was tasked with delivering it to a customer as part of our pick-up and drop service. But on his way, the car met with a serious accident. Gopala was only slightly injured, but the car—a brand new one—was completely damaged. The customer has demanded a replacement, and we've settled with them by providing a new car."

"Go on," Shastry said, his fingers lightly tapping the desk.

"Now, the issue is the money. After insurance claims, there's still a shortfall of Rs. 75,000.00, and we also want to penalize Gopala Rs. 25,000.00 for reckless driving. The company's asking me to draft an agreement and an indemnity bond with him, stating that we'll deduct the amount from his salary."

Shastry raised an eyebrow, leaning back in his chair. "You're talking about a total of Rs. 1 lakh. And how much does Gopala earn?"

"Rs. 13,000 a month."

Shastry let out a soft sigh. "So, your company expects this boy to pay back such a huge amount over time? That's nearly a year of his salary gone." Pramod nodded hesitantly. "I understand, sir, but business is business. The management thinks he should be held accountable."

Shastry's gaze narrowed and his voice became firmer but still kind. "Pramod, I understand your position. But is it really fair to burden such a young boy with this kind of financial strain? He's just starting his life, barely earning enough to support himself. What kind of message does it send if we punish employees so harshly for accidents that could happen to anyone?"

Pramod looked uncomfortable, shifting in his seat. "But sir, we have to follow company policy. These are not easy times for the business."

Shastry leaned forward, his voice lowering. "And how do you expect the company to run without your workers? Without people like Gopala, who are the backbones of operations? You can't crush them under the weight of these penalties and expect them to function. Their welfare should be a priority—otherwise, how will any factory, industry, or service station run smoothly?"

Pramod rubbed the back of his neck. "I see your point, sir. But the management—"

"Convince them," Shastry interrupted; his eyes sharp. "Convince them to withdraw the claims against Gopala. Let the insurance cover the damage, and instead, help him recover. Give him a little more money to get back on his feet. That's how you'll build loyalty and respect in your workforce."

There was a long pause. Pramod's face hardened, and the hesitation was gone. "With respect, Mr. Shastry, I'm not here for advice on how to manage the service station. You run a small office that was once a garage and I doubt you understand the challenges of running a business like mine. I need you to draft the agreement and the bond, and that's all."

Shastry studied him for a moment, his expression unreadable. Then, with a slow nod, he simply said, "Very well. Come back in the evening. I'll have the documents ready." That evening, Pramod Kumar returned, still looking a bit agitated. Shastry was waiting for him, sitting casually behind his desk.

"Here are the documents," Shastry said, sliding the agreement and indemnity bond across the table. "It's all drafted as per your instructions." Pramod picked up the documents and started flipping through them, his mind preoccupied with the task. But before he could finish reviewing, Shastry slid a second sheet across the desk—an Invoice!

Pramod glanced down and froze. His eyes widened as he read the figure—Rs. 40,000.00!

"What is this?!" Pramod exclaimed. "Forty thousand? For drafting two agreements? That's preposterous!"

Shastry smiled, his tone casual but with an edge. "It's not preposterous. It's the cost of my knowledge. You see, Pramod, when you look at a man, don't just see his showroom—see the godown inside. I charge for my thoughts, my expertise. And this fee, it's non-negotiable."

Pramod's face flushed with frustration. "This is outrageous! I thought Supreeth said you'd be reasonable."

"I am being reasonable, Pramod. You came to me for professional help. And you've got the best advice, even though you chose to ignore it. The fee is payable immediately." Shastry's voice was calm but firm.

There was a tense silence, the weight of Shastry's words hanging in the air. Pramod grumbled but finally pulled out the money from his bag and handed over the amount.

Shastry reached out to collect the fee with a polite smile. "Thank you."

Pramod, still fuming, collected the documents and stormed out, muttering under his breath.

A few minutes after Pramod left, Shastry reached into his pocket and picked up his phone and dialed a number.

"Gopala?"

"Yes, sir?" came the hesitant voice on the other end.

"I need you and your close workmates to come to my office right away. It's important."

About an hour later, Gopala and two of his friends entered the small office, their faces tense and anxious. "Sir, did something happen? Is there more legal trouble?" Gopala asked, his voice filled with worry.

Shastry smiled and shook his head. "No, no, nothing to worry." He stood up, walking over to the three young men, and placed the envelope into Gopala's hands.

"This is for you. Rs.35,000.00"

Gopala blinked, his mouth falling open in shock. "W-what? But... why?" "Because no one should be punished for an accident and certainly not someone who works as hard as you do for so little. I've taken care of the situation. This is your money—use it to recover and get back on your feet."

Tears welled up in Gopala's eyes as he clutched the envelope. His colleagues looked on in disbelief, but soon their expressions softened into gratitude.

"Sir, I can't... this is too much..." Gopala stammered, overcome with emotion. "It's not too much, Gopala. It's what's fair," Shastry said softly.

Word spread quickly among Gopala's colleagues at the service station. That same evening, about 50 employees gathered at a nearby park, close to Shastry's office. They all knew what had happened—how their colleague had been helped by a lawyer who understood more than just the law.

The employees resolved to contribute a day's salary each toward Gopala's welfare. They passed around a collection box, gathering money far in excess of what Gopala needed.

In the presence of Shastry, they handed the remaining money to Gopala, who stood there with tears in his eyes, overwhelmed by the support and compassion from his coworkers.

And all of them—every single one—turned to Shastry with gratitude.

"Thank you, sir, for showing us the way," one of the senior employees said, shaking Shastry's hand. "It's because of you that we realized how much we need to stand by each other. Gopala's not just a worker, he's one of us. And you made us see that."

Shastry, with his usual modest smile, simply nodded. "It's not about the money. It's about recognizing the value of the people who help build our lives. Gopala is part of your family, and no family lets one of their own fall behind."

The small gathering in the park was filled with quiet moments of reflection, the employees exchanging words of encouragement with Gopala, who could barely hold back his emotions. It wasn't just about the money anymore—it was about the solidarity, the community spirit, and the realization that they weren't alone in this harsh world of work and struggle.

As the sun set, casting a warm glow over the park, the employees slowly dispersed, many of them giving Shastry one last thankful nod as they left.

Shastry returned to his office, a slight breeze following him as he pushed open the creaky door. He hadn't expected the evening to turn out this way, but it filled him with a quiet sense of satisfaction. These were the moments that reminded him why he had chosen this profession—not for the money, but for the people.

Just as he was about to settle down at his desk to look over some pending files, he noticed someone waiting at the door.

A tall man with a salt-and-pepper beard stood there, hands behind his back, his posture tense but patient. His eyes were sharp, scanning the office as if measuring the man inside it.

"Good evening, Mr. Shastry," the man said, his voice calm but with a slight edge. "I hope I'm not intruding. My name is Nair. I've been waiting for you."

Shastry raised an eyebrow, intrigued by the man's introduction and demeanor.

"Not at all, Mr. Nair," Shastry said, gesturing toward the chair opposite his desk. "Please, have a seat. What brings you here?"

Nair took a seat; his movements deliberate and slow, as if weighing every action carefully. "I have a case that requires someone like you—a man who understands."

Shastry folded his hands on the desk, sensing that this conversation was about to take him down a very different path.

Nair looked older than his years, the worries of life etched deeply on his face. He wiped the sweat from his brow before taking a seat.

"Yes, please sit. What brings you here?" Shastry asked, leaning back slightly, intrigued by the man's unease.

Nair took a deep breath, and his voice trembled slightly as he spoke. "I run a small plastic materials business, Mr. Shastry, nothing too big. Just enough to get by. But I'm here because of my son... Mahesh!"

Shastry raised an eyebrow, his interest piqued. "Go on," Shastry encouraged, his voice calm but his focus sharpening.

Nair's hands trembled as he tried to explain. "Mahesh... he's only 19. His mother, Padma, and I... we weren't married. He's the result of an affair. I've tried to support them as best as I can, sending them what little money I could, but I couldn't be there for them like a proper father should." Nair's voice cracked, and he shifted uncomfortably in his chair.

"And now?" Shastry asked softly, sensing the weight of the story yet to come.

Nair lowered his gaze, guilt written across his face. "Now, Mahesh is in real trouble. He's fallen in with Contractor Krishna and his gang. Last week... there was an incident. My boy—he... attacked our landlord, Prakash Gowda, in broad daylight, in full view of the public. And now, Inspector Sridhar is hunting him down like an animal."

Shastry's eyes narrowed slightly as he sat up. "Why hasn't Prakash Gowda filed a complaint?"

"He's scared of Mahesh and the gang," Nair said, his voice barely a whisper. "But Sridhar isn't the kind to let something like this slide. If he finds Mahesh, I'm sure he'll beat him within an inch of his life."

Shastry paused, his mind racing. Mahesh—young, misguided, but not a hardened criminal. He had been pulled into the wrong crowd, and now his life was on the line.

"Where is Mahesh now?" Shastry asked.

"He's hiding," Nair said quickly, his voice shaking. "I've got him staying with a friend in Ramnagara. But it's only a matter of time before Sridhar's men find him. I'm here, Mr. Shastry, because I don't know where else to turn. I need you to help my son."

Shastry's gaze softened. He could see the desperation in Nair's eyes—the plea of a father who felt he had failed his son.

"Bring him here, to my office, first thing tomorrow morning," Shastry said. "But make sure he comes in disguise. We can't risk anyone seeing him."

Nair nodded, relief flooding his face. "I'll bring him. Thank you, Mr. Shastry."

The next morning, Shastry was at Ramesh's shop by 6:00 a.m., for a cuppa, with the faint smell of cigarettes wafting through the air. The small shop was already bustling with its early regulars, and Ramesh, the ever-cheerful owner, grinned as he handed Shastry a cup.

"You're early today, Mr. Shastry," Ramesh chuckled, wiping his hands on his apron. "What's the occasion? Haven't seen you here this early in months!"

Shastry smiled slightly, taking a drag from his cigarette. "Case and Clients Ramesha."

Ramesh leaned forward, lowering his voice in a conspiratorial tone. "Must be something serious if it's got you out of bed at this hour. You're not even in your uniform"

Shastry let out a quiet laugh, shaking his head. "You know me too well, Ramesh."

"Well, if anyone can fix a mess, it's you, Mr. Shastry," Ramesh said, nodding with a sage-like expression. "What'll it be today? Tea? Biscuit? Banana?"

Shastry grinned. "You know the routine but I'll have a strong coffee instead of tea!"

After finishing his small breakfast, Shastry stubbed out his cigarette, paid Ramesh, and walked back to his office. His mind was already gearing up for what lay ahead.

When he arrived, he found Nair and Mahesh already waiting outside, Mahesh's head covered with a scarf to disguise his appearance.

"Morning, sir," Nair said, his voice tight with worry.

"Come in quickly," Shastry said, motioning for them to enter.

Inside the office, Shastry handed Mahesh a vakalathnama—a document authorizing Shastry to represent him. Mahesh hesitated for a moment before picking up the pen, his hand trembling as he signed.

"You're in safe hands now, Mahesha," Shastry said calmly. "Now, tell me everything. I need to know exactly what happened."

Mahesh swallowed hard, his voice barely above a whisper. "It was Prakash Gowda... he—he hurt my mother. She was humiliated in front of everyone. I lost control... I... I beat him." His voice broke, and tears filled his eyes.

Shastry remained silent, waiting for Mahesh to continue. The young boy's pain was palpable, and it filled the room like a heavy fog.

"I didn't mean to hurt him that badly," Mahesh said, tears streaming down his face. "I just wanted him to know what it felt like to be powerless. Like how he made my mother feel. But now... now I'm a criminal. I didn't mean for any of this to happen."

Shastry's eyes softened with understanding. He had seen many cases where young men, pushed by desperation, ended up in situations far worse than they could handle. Mahesh wasn't a hardened criminal—he was a boy, lost in a world he didn't understand.

Shastry reached across the desk, his hand resting lightly on Mahesh's. "Listen, Mahesha. You've made mistakes, but you're not beyond saving. This is the system we live in, and sometimes it's cruel. But we'll figure this out. You have to trust me."

Mahesh nodded, still wiping away tears. Nair, sitting beside him, placed a hand on his son's shoulder, his own eyes filled with guilt and pain.

Shastry stood up, his voice now taking on a tone of command. "For now, you both need to keep a low profile. Stay hidden. Don't make any contact with anyone until we've secured bail. This will take a couple of weeks, but I'll make sure you're safe."

Nair and Mahesh nodded, grateful for Shastry's calm assurance.

"Thank you, Mr. Shastry." Nair's voice was thick with emotion. "I don't know what we would have done without you."

Shastry gave them a reassuring nod. "We'll take it one step at a time. Just stay quiet and let me do my job. We'll talk again soon."

Tales Of Lawyer Ramachandra Shastry

As Nair and Mahesh left the office, Shastry stood by the window, watching them disappear into the early morning streets. He lit another cigarette, the smoke curling upwards as he thought about the case that lay ahead.

The clock was ticking. Inspector Sridhar was no fool, and the longer Mahesh remained hidden, the more aggressive the police search would become.

But Shastry was ready. He was always ready.

The early morning sun streamed through the thin curtains of Shastry's office, casting a soft glow on the cluttered desk. The sounds of Bengaluru's bustling streets echoed faintly outside as Shastry, now settled behind his old wooden desk, lit a cigarette and leaned back in his chair. He had done this many times earlier, today was no different. But this was Mahesh's lifeline. A single mistake could mean the young boy's future would be consumed by a criminal system that was both harsh and unforgiving.

Shastry knew the stakes were high. Inspector Sridhar was no ordinary officer. His reputation for building watertight cases preceded him, and Shastry had a feeling that Sridhar was intent on using Mahesh as a scapegoat in Contractor Krishna's case. The fact that Sridhar had lodged the FIR without identifying Mahesh by name made it clear— Mahesh was the "unknown person" mentioned in the FIR, and Sridhar planned to implicate him later.

But Shastry wasn't about to let that happen. He took a long drag of his cigarette, letting the smoke linger in the air, and turned his attention to the blank paper in front of him. Section 438 of the Criminal Procedure Code— Anticipatory Bail. Shastry had studied this provision meticulously, knowing it could mean the difference between freedom and imprisonment for his client.

The case at hand was the assault which took place in Chandu Lal's shop by Contractor Krishna and his gang for the offences punishable under sections 143, 147, 148, 448, 427, 307 and 149 of the Indian Penal Code, 1860. All the gang members including Contractor Krishna, Naga, Seena, Abbu, TK, Kothi and Kulla had been arrested barring one unknown boy who was none other than Mahesh. Seena and Kothi had been enlarged on bail on special conditions owing to their sympathetic concessions under the differently abled category.

Shastry opened his well-worn casebook, flipping through the pages filled with landmark judgments that wouldserve as the foundation for his arguments. Shastry had always been a meticulous lawyer, believing that most part of the law was about knowing statutes, precedents and more importantly the intentions behind it.

Shastry began by penning the first few lines, setting the stage for the bail plea.

"In the Court of the District Sessions Judge, at Bengaluru..."

His handwriting was steady, his mind racing through the complexities of the case as he drafted the preamble.

"The word "Anticipatory Bail" under Section 438 of Cr.P.C., although widely accepted, is a misnomer," Shastry muttered to himself as he wrote. He knew that thegeneral public often misunderstood it as it represents a futility that bail may be granted by the court in apprehension of an arrest., and believe it to be a preemptive right.

But Shastry knew better—it was meant for specific circumstances where the arrest was likely, and the person had a reasonable belief that the authorities were looking to arrest him in a non-bailable offense; then if at all such a person is arrested for such an offence, then he may be enlarged on bail.

"Reason to believe," he whispered, underlining the phrase as he wrote. He paused, reflecting on the intentions of Sridhar.

Shastry leaned back and tapped the paper lightly with his pen, focusing on constructing his primary arguments. He knew that clarity and precision were keys to swaying the judge's opinion.

The first ground he penned was identity.

"1. The identity of the accused is in question."

"The FIR has been lodged against an 'unknown person,' and as such, no overt acts can be attributed directly to the petitioner, Mahesh. The police are merely assuming his involvement based on vague suspicions and hearsay. There has been no mention about the involvement of the boy by Lal or any other eye witnesses. The petitioner has not been implicated by any witnesses, nor have any specific allegations been made in the FIR that Mahesh took part in the criminal activities. There are no eyewitnesses who can confirm his role in the alleged assault or conspiracy."

Shastry paused for a moment, thinking about how best to frame the next ground. He wanted the judge to see that there were no direct actions linking Mahesh to the crime. Sridhar had failed to identify Mahesh, which meant there was no concrete evidence to pin the crime on him.

"2. No overt acts attributed to the Petitioner."

"According to the complaint the grievous injury caused was primarily due to the assault caused by Krishna. Mahesh neither had the intention of causing harm in order to kill Chandu Lal nor did he attack and cause the injury to Lal. The grievous injury sustained by the victim was purportedly caused by the prime accused, Contractor Krishna, who is already secured in judicial custody. The petitioner had no involvement in the physical attack."

Shastry took a deep breath, knowing this was a critical point. He moved to the third ground—parity.

"3. Parity with co-accused who have been granted bail."

He carefully worded this section, knowing that judges often relied on the principle of parity to ensure fairness. "Two other accused in the same case have already been enlarged on bail. Given that the petitioner's involvement is far less significant, and he was not named in the FIR, he is entitled to bail on the grounds of parity."

As Shastry wrote, his mind worked in overdrive. He moved to the next ground, where he could firmly differentiate Mahesh's role from Contractor Krishna.

This was one of the most vital parts of his application. He wanted to make it clear that Mahesh, while present, was not directly involved in the assault that caused the grievous injury. Krishna was the main player, and Shastry needed the court to see that.

Finally, he came to the fourth ground—cooperation and conditions.

"4. The petitioner is ready to abide by all conditions imposed by the Hon'ble Court."

"Mahesh is prepared to fully cooperate with the ongoing investigation. He has no prior criminal record and is not a flight risk. The petitioner submits that he will appear before the Investigating Officer as and when required. He shall furnish solvent sureties to the Court to ensure regular appearance."

Shastry knew this would be the clincher—showing the judge that Mahesh wasn't a hardened criminal that he was willing to cooperate and wouldn't abscond. Judges were more likely to grant bail if they believed the accused would adhere to the court's conditions.

As Shastry put down his pen, he re-read the entire notes. Each word was carefully chosen, each argument laid out with precision. He leaned back in his chair, satisfied with the first draft but still thinking about the arguments he would make in court. In so far as the assault on Prakash Gowda was concerned, there was no complaint and as such there was no necessity for any bail.

He took another drag of his cigarette, letting the smoke swirl in the dim light of the office.

Suddenly, the door opened slightly, and Ramesh peeked in. "Ah, Mr. Shastry, another cigarette? You'll burn through your lungs before you finish your next case!"

Shastry chuckled, putting out the cigarette. "I'll take my chances, Ramesha."

Ramesh came in with his usual banter, placing a cup of tea on the desk. "So, what's this big case you're working on, eh? Some dangerous criminal again?"

Shastry smirked, not wanting to reveal too much. "Let's just say, Ramesha, this one's complicated."

Ramesh grinned. "Complicated? I thought you were the best in the game, Shastry! There's nothing you can't solve."

Shastry smiled, shaking his head. "Flattery won't get you more tips, Ramesha. But thanks for the coffee."

As Ramesh left, Shastry stood and paced the office, thinking about the upcoming tasks ahead: Final draft, printing, arranging all the annexure in paginated order and indexing, stitching, filing, scrutiny and then hearing finally. He knew Sridhar would try to oppose the bail with every ounce of his strength he could muster, but Shastry was ready. Or was he??

Inside, the small, cluttered space of Shastry's law office, was filled with the hum of an aging second-hand desktop that sounded more like an aircraft preparing for takeoff. Shastry sat behind his desk, furiously typing away at the keyboard, his fingers moving swiftly as he composed the anticipatory bail application of Mahesha in the matter pertaining to attack on Chandu Lal.

At least, that's what he hoped to be doing. In reality, the computer was taking its own sweet time to process the simplest of commands, and the screen was frozen on the infamous spinning circle—the wheel of doom. "Come on…" Shastry muttered under his breath, hitting the Enter key repeatedly. His patience, much like his desktop, was nearing its end.

Across the room, his fourth-hand laser printer, a relic of a bygone era, sat ominously like a grumpy old man who had seen too much. Its buttons were worn, the plastic yellowed with age, and every time Shastry tried to print, it made a noise that could only be described as the sound of a dying walrus.

"Just one last page printout. Is that too much to ask?" Shastry sighed, standing up and walking over to the printer, which was currently wheezing out a half-printed page at the speed of a tortoise. He banged it lightly, hoping it would get the message. "I should have just written this application by hand. This thing belongs in a museum!"

As if to mock him further, the two ancient speakers attached to the desktop suddenly came to life, blaring out a loud, distorted notification sound that startled Shastry so badly he knocked over a stack of legal books. "Aaaargh!" he yelped, clutching his chest. "These damn speakers! I swear they're possessed!"

The sound they emitted was supposed to indicate that the print job was done. Instead, it sounded more like someone screaming through a tin can. He walked over to the desktop, glaring at the speakers as if they were co-conspirators in his technological torment.

"I'll have to buy a laptop and a printer soon! A sleek, shiny laptop, no wires, no drama, just peace and a fast, easy to use economical Lazer printer." Shastry muttered to himself, staring dreamily into the distance. His fantasy of holding a brand-new laptop was the only thing that kept him from chucking the old desktop out the window.

Turning his attention back to the printer, Shastry sighed in frustration. The half-printed page was stuck, and the machine had gone into a kind of meditative state, refusing to acknowledge any further commands.

"You've served your time, old friend, but this... this is betrayal," Shastry said dramatically, addressing the printer as if it were a retired warrior who had let him down in battle. He pulled the paper, which came out in shreds, the text barely legible.

He stared at the torn half of the legal document in his hands and then at the printer, which blinked a single light in defiance.

"Oh, so you think you're clever, huh?" Shastry muttered, rolling up his sleeves like he was about to engage in a physical fight. He hit the on/off switch again, this time slamming it harder.

The printer groaned back to life but decided to exact revenge by printing out copies of a document Shastry had printed three days ago. The same page kept rolling out, one after another, all completely useless. "This is how you want to play it, huh?" Shastry yelled, snatching up the freshly printed copies and shaking them in frustration. "I only need one copy, not an entire anthology!"

As if it were in cahoots with the printer, the desktop decided this was the perfect time to freeze again. Shastry hurried back to the desk, jabbing the mouse furiously. The cursor had vanished, replaced by yet another spinning circle.

"Fantastic. Just fantastic!" he groaned, leaning back in his chair, eyes closed. "I should've been a doctor. They don't need desktops for surgeries. They don't deal with this kind of nonsense."

The speakers crackled again, letting out a random burst of static, as if to mock him further.

"I get it, I get it! You're all against me!" Shastry shouted, throwing his hands up in the air. "But you won't win. I'll get this application printed if it's the last thing I do!"

Shastry leaned forward, tapping the desk thoughtfully. "One day," he muttered. "It'll be just me, a high-speed machine, and... peace."

He imagined it—the sleek, thin body of a laptop in his hands, the gentle hum of a working machine, the freedom of typing without fear of technical betrayal. The dream seemed far away, but it was the only thing keeping him from losing his mind. For now, though, he was stuck with the desktop, the speakers, and the printer that seemed determined to ruin his life.

He glanced at the half-printed page still stuck in the printer. With a sigh, he sat back down, glancing toward the ceiling.

"Maybe I'll just... write the whole thing by hand," he muttered. "After all, Gandhi didn't have a desktop, and he did pretty well."

The speakers let out another burst of static, and Shastry shot them a glare. "Keep it up, and I'll donate you to the scrapyard along with your friend the printer." With that, he rushed to a nearby computer center to complete the process of printing the bail application.

Back in the office with all the necessary papers in hand, the air was thick with the familiar scent of cigarettes and old paper, as he sat hunched over his desk, his fingers deftly maneuvering a green thread through the needle.

In front of him lay the bail application he had so meticulously drafted—its pages arranged in perfect order, ready to be bound in the official style. But this was the tricky part. Stitching the pages together was an art form, one that junior lawyers like him had to master early in their careers. And it wasn't just about formality—it was about showing respect for the legal system.

"Green thread... check. Needle... check," Shastry muttered to himself, threading the needle carefully. "Just have to get this thing stitched, and then it's off to the court."

The needle pierced through the first few pages smoothly, and for a brief moment, Shastry felt like he was making progress. His ancient printer had miraculously spat out the required documents, and now he was just one stitch away from filing the bail application.

But just as he was about to complete the final stitch, the needle slipped—straight into his finger.

"Aaaargh!" Shastry yelped, dropping the needle as blood oozed from his finger.

"Perfect. Just perfect," he groaned, shaking his hand. The sharp pain of the poke made him wince, but worse was the sight of a small red blotch now forming on the last page of the application.

"Brilliant, just what I needed." He grabbed his kerchief, pressing it to his finger as he examined the damage. "Maybe I should start charging for 'blood, sweat, and tears,'" he muttered, half-laughing at his misfortune as he wiped the blotch away.

With a few more careful stitches, Shastry finally bound the pages together. The bail application was ready— stitched and sealed in proper legal form. He sat back, satisfied with his work despite the small band-aid now wrapped around his throbbing finger.

Next day, Shastry arrived at the City Court Complex, his bag slung over his shoulder, the bail application clutched in hand like a prized artifact. Filing paperwork in court was always a mixed bag—sometimes things went smoothly, other times it felt like the entire system was conspiring against you. He approached the court filing counter, where a bored-looking clerk sat behind a thick pane of glass. The clerk barely looked up as Shastry slid the bundle of papers across the counter.

The clerk glanced at the papers, flipping through them at a speed that made Shastry nervous. Would he find a flaw? Was the stitching done right? He held his breath as the clerk checked for signatures, peered at the process fees, and finally stamped the top page with a loud thud. He passed on the file to another clerk who made an entry in the register and said "Criminal Miscellaneous Petition

No. 3121/10" The clerk scribbled something down and handed the papers back through the window. "Court Hall No. 67. Your hearing is listed tomorrow."

Shastry breathed a sigh of relief. "Thank you."

The filing had gone through without a hitch, and the case had been assigned. He couldn't help but smile as he walked out of the filing counter—so far, so good.

The next morning, Shastry arrived at Court Hall No. 67 with a renewed sense of confidence. He had been in front of Judge Shankar a few times before and knew the man's reputation well. Shankar was a seasoned judge, known for his patience with junior lawyers and his genuine interest in helping them develop their legal acumen. But that didn't mean Shankar was an easy judge. He expected junior lawyers to be prepared, and Shastry knew that a well-argued case could earn him praise from the bench.

As he entered the courtroom, he glanced around. The room was already packed with lawyers, clerks, and accused persons, each waiting for their moment before the judge. The smell of freshly starched robes filled the air, and Shastry felt a small jolt of excitement.

His case, Criminal Miscellaneous Petition No. 3121/2010, was listed at Sl. No. 27, giving him just enough time to prepare his arguments.

At precisely 11:00 a.m., Judge Shankar entered the courtroom. The attender's loud voice rang out, "Silence!"

Shastry stood respectfully as the judge took his seat, his face calm and collected, yet alert. Shankar's gaze swept over the courtroom, and the room seemed to settle into a hushed silence.

One by one, the cases were called out, and finally, the bench clerk called, "C.M.P No. 3121/2010, Mahesh vs. State of Karnataka."

Shastry stood, adjusting his blazer, feeling the nervous anticipation creeping up his spine. This was it. The moment where all his hard work would either pay off or crumble.

He stepped forward, his voice steady but commanding. "May it please Your Lordship, the petitioner Mahesh seeks anticipatory bail under Section 438 of the Criminal Procedure Code."

Judge Shankar nodded, gesturing for him to continue.

"The allegations against my client are vague, Your Honor, and there are no overt acts directly attributing to my client in the alleged crime." Shastry began, his words carefully chosen. He wanted to lay out the facts with precision, without getting carried away with rhetoric.

"The police have registered an FIR against Contractor Krishna and several others for an alleged assault. However, my client, Mahesh, is not named in the FIR. His identity is simply listed as 'unknown,' and there is no evidence to suggest that he was involved in the crime."

Shankar leaned back in his chair, his expression thoughtful. Shastry could feel the judge's focus on him.

"Furthermore, Your Honor, the primary accused, Contractor Krishna, is already in judicial custody. It is my submission that Mahesh, a young man with no previous criminal record, is being wrongly implicated simply because of his association with Krishna."

Shastry paused, glancing at the public prosecutor, Himanand Kumar, who was shifting slightly in his seat, preparing to counter. But Shastry wasn't done yet.

"Your Honor, two other accused in the same case have already been granted bail on similar grounds. I submit that my client is equally entitled to bail on the principle of parity.

Judge Shankar gave a brief nod, acknowledging Shastry's arguments. Shastry stood confidently, waiting for the public prosecutor's turn.

Himanand Kumar, a veteran prosecutor with years of experience, rose slowly from his seat. He was known for his deliberate manner and his tendency to ask for adjournments when cornered.

"My Lord, I seek a short adjournment," Himanand Kumar said in his deep voice. "I need to take instructions from the Investigating Officer, Inspector Sridhar, before I can proceed with my arguments."

Shastry inwardly sighed. An adjournment request wasn't surprising—public prosecutors often did this to buy more time.

Judge Shankar glanced at Himanand, then at Shastry.

"Very well, Mr. Kumar, you have two days." The judge made a quick note, his pen moving smoothly across the file. "The matter is adjourned to the day after tomorrow."

Shastry bowed slightly in acknowledgment. "Obliged, Your Honor."

As the court adjourned, Shastry felt a mix of anticipation and tension building inside him. The first step had gone well, but the real battle lay ahead. As he walked out of the courtroom, he allowed himself a small smile. There was hope.

The day of reckoning was a bright morning in Bengaluru, but inside Court Hall No. 67, the air was thick with anticipation. The room was crowded, as always, with junior and senior lawyers, clerks, and anxious litigants waiting for their cases to be heard. The familiar shuffle of papers, the rustling of robes, and the quiet murmur of voices filled the space as Judge Sri Shankar presided from the bench.

The previous day's adjournment had left Ramachandra Shastry with a sense of nervous energy. Today was different. Criminal Miscellaneous Petition No. 3121/2010, filed on behalf of Mahesh, was listed at Sl. No. 34, and the stakes couldn't be higher.

Shastry knew the opposing argument was going to be tough—Public Prosecutor Himanand Kumar wasn't one to go down without a fight. He had a reputation for solid arguments and an even more solid delivery in court. Shastry, though confident in his preparation, was still wary. He had seen too many cases swing in unpredictable directions.

By the time Case No. 34 was called, the courtroom had settled into a tense silence.

"C.M.P. No. 3121/2010, Mahesh vs. State of Karnataka." The bench clerk's voice cut through the murmurs, and Shastry stood, adjusting his coat as he moved toward the podium.

On the other side, Himanand Kumar stood tall, his expression calm and calculating, a thick file of objections under his arm. Judge Shankar nodded, motioning for Himanand to begin.

"May it please Your Lordship," Himanand Kumar began, his voice steady but commanding, "I stand here today to oppose the anticipatory bail application filed on behalf of the petitioner, Mahesh. My objections, as outlined indetail in the written submission, are based on four specific grounds."

Shastry watched Himanand carefully, aware of the prosecutor's methodical approach. He had seen this before—Himanand liked to build his case slowly, like a hunter setting a trap, ensuring that when he made his final point, it would land with full impact.

"First and foremost, Your Honor," Himanand continued, flipping through his file for emphasis, "the petitioner, Mahesh, is a flight risk. We have information, though unofficial, that Mahesh has strong connections to criminal elements. If this court grants him the leniency of anticipatory bail, there is every reason to believe that he will abscond. We have already seen signs that Mahesh has been in hiding ever since the incident with Contractor Krishna. It is highly likely that he will evade the law if released."

Himanand let that point settle into the courtroom, his eyes briefly glancing at Shastry, a slight challenge in them.

"Secondly, Your Honor," Himanand said, pausing a little, as was his habit, "though there have been no formal complaints lodged, we have credible information that Mahesh has been involved in other offenses. The only reason these incidents have not been registered is due to the complainants being too afraid to come forward. Contractor Krishna and his associates, including Mahesh, have instilled fear in the local community, silencing potential witnesses."

Shastry's jaw tightened, knowing that this was a speculative argument, but it was crafted well enough to make an impression on the judge. Judge Shankar, however, maintained his neutral expression, nodding slightly but giving nothing away.

"Thirdly, Your Honor," Himanand continued, his voice taking on a sharper tone, "Mahesh is not the innocent person his counsel portrays him to be. His association with Krishna's gang has already stained his character. The court should not overlook the fact that his mere presence in this gang makes him complicit in criminal activities. He is dangerous—not only to the public but also to those who might testify against him."

Shastry felt a knot forming in his stomach. He knew the public perception of Mahesh was already skewed because of his association with the gang, and Himanand was playing into that fear.

"And finally," Himanand said, lowering his voice slightly, a note of somberness entering his tone, "keeping Mahesh in incarceration would provide him the opportunity to reform. He is still young, Your Honor, and while we acknowledge that he may not have played a central role in the crimes, his time in custody could help him mend his ways. By granting him bail, this court risks allowing him to fall deeper into criminal activities."

There was a moment of silence in the courtroom as Himanand Kumar closed his file, letting his arguments sink in. Judge Shankar leaned back in his chair, considering the points laid before him.

Shastry, standing with his arms behind his back, exhaled slowly. He knew Himanand's arguments were solid, but they were based on assumptions and possibilities, not concrete facts. That was his opening, and he would use it to turn the tide.

Judge Shankar finally spoke, his tone neutral but curious. "Mr. Kumar, these are serious objections, but they seem to rely heavily on conjecture. You've mentioned other offenses, but no complaints. You've labeled the petitioner a flight risk, yet there's no evidence of an attempt to flee. Can you substantiate these claims further?"

Himanand nodded. "Your Honor, while we don't have a formal record of Mahesh's prior offenses, the fact that no complaints were lodged is telling. It indicates the fear that he and Krishna's gang have spread in the community. As for the flight risk, his association with criminal elements who have the resources to facilitate his escape is enough reason for caution. I urge this court to consider the larger picture."

Shastry stepped forward, his mind racing but his exterior calm, the file of his own submissions in hand. His heart pounded, but he knew this was the moment that could make or break the case.

"May it please Your Lordship," Shastry began, his voice clear and firm. "The objections raised by the prosecution, while thoroughly presented, are based largely on assumptions and unverified information. The lack of formal complaints, which my learned friend has used to paint my client as a menace, is not evidence of guilt. Rather, it points to the weakness in the prosecution's case. If Mahesh had truly committed these offenses, why haven't these so-called complainants come forward?"

Shastry paused, letting the question hang in the air, watching Judge Shankar for a reaction. The judge's face remained passive, but Shastry could tell he was listening intently.

"As for the claim that my client is a flight risk," Shastry continued, "Your Honor, Mahesh has not attempted to flee the jurisdiction. In fact, his whereabouts have been known since the incident occurred, and he has remained in close contact with his family. The mere fact that someone is associated with an unsavory character does not make them a criminal. By that logic, we could imprison anyone who's ever had a cup of tea with the wrong person."

A few chuckles rose from the back of the courtroom, but Shastry's expression remained serious. He glanced at Himanand Kumar, who had stiffened slightly, clearly not pleased with the tone of Shastry's argument.

"The prosecution would have this court believe that my client is a hardened criminal, but the truth is that Mahesh is a young man who got involved with the wrong crowd. He is not a danger to society, and his presence in jail will do nothing to reform him—it will only ruin him further."

Shastry could feel the momentum shifting, but he wasn't done yet.

"Furthermore, Your Honor," he said, his voice gaining strength, "the principle of parity applies here. Two co-accused, who were alleged to have committed more serious offenses than Mahesh, have already been granted bail. It would be unjust to deny my client the same relief, especially when there is no direct evidence linking him to any violent act."

Shastry knew this was his moment to delve into the sacred principles of the law, the ones that guided judges and lawyers across the country. He straightened his robe, adjusted his glasses slightly, and began.

"Your Lordship, the provision for anticipatory bail under Section 438 of the Criminal Procedure Code is one that has been debated and discussed at length by the Supreme Court of India. It is not merely a procedural safeguard; it is a protection of personal liberty, as enshrined under Article 21 of the Constitution. The sacred nature of this provision has been upheld by our highest court in several landmark judgments, which I would like to place before this Hon'ble Court."

The tension in the room heightened. Even Public Prosecutor Himanand Kumar, who had been firm in his opposition, leaned forward slightly in his chair, listening closely.

Shastry took a deep breath and began, his voice steady and firm.

"The most foundational case that guides the understanding of anticipatory bail is the celebrated judgment in the case of Gurbaksh Singh Sibbia vs. State of Punjab." He paused, letting the name of the case sink in before continuing.

"In this case, Your Lordship, the Supreme Court laid down that the power to grant anticipatory bail is an extraordinary one and should be exercised sparingly, but at the same time, it is a tool to protect individual liberty. The court in *Sibbia* emphasized that anticipatory bail should not be denied merely because the petitioner is accused of a serious offense. The gravity of the offense is not the sole factor to determine whether bail should be granted or not."

Judge Shankar nodded slightly, recognizing the significance of Sibbia. Shastry continued, his voice growing more confident.

"The Supreme Court further held that the provision of anticipatory bail was introduced as a measure to protect individuals from the possibility of arrest on frivolous or trumped-up charges, ensuring that no individual suffers unnecessary humiliation at the hands of the authorities. This is precisely the case we are dealing with here, Your Honor. The identity of my client, Mahesh, is under question. There are no overt acts attributed to him in the crime, and yet the fear of arrest looms large over his head."

Shastry could feel the courtroom hanging on to his every word. He had carefully chosen Gurbaksh Singh Sibbia as the starting point to establish the principle of fairness.

"Your Lordship, in the recent case of Siddharam Satlingappa Mhetre vs. State of Maharashtra, the Supreme Court reiterated the sacred nature of anticipatory bail. It stated clearly that 'the personal liberty of an individual is the most cherished and valued right guaranteed under the Constitution.'"

His voice rang out clearly across the courtroom, echoing the very words of the Supreme Court.

"In Mhetre, the Supreme court held that the mere registration of an FIR or the possibility of being named in the charge sheet should not be sufficient grounds to deny anticipatory bail. There must be specific reasons to believe that the accused would misuse the liberty granted by the court. In our case, Your Lordship, the prosecution has failed to provide any such specific reason."

Shastry's gaze flicked briefly to Himanand Kumar, who had now stopped taking notes and was watching Shastry intently.

"In fact, the Supreme Court in Mhetre went further to assert that anticipatory bail is a remedy to ensure that the liberty of a person is not compromised purely based on suspicion or mere accusations. It ensures that people like my client, Mahesh, do not suffer the trauma of arrest for a crime they are yet to be convicted of, especially when there is no substantial evidence against them."

Shastry wasn't done yet. He moved forward, presenting his next argument with confidence.

"Another important case, Your Lordship, is Balchand Jain vs. State of Madhya Pradesh, where the Supreme Court clarified that anticipatory bail must be granted when there are 'reasonable grounds' for believing that the person has been falsely implicated or that the accusations are baseless. It stressed that anticipatory bail serves as a safeguard for people who are likely to be victimized by the police or influential parties."

He turned his gaze back to Judge Shankar, making sure to keep his tone respectful but assertive.

"In the present case, Your Honor, the petitioner Mahesh is in danger of being falsely implicated by the prosecution especially Inspector Sridhar, who has yet to provide any clear evidence tying Mahesh to the crime. The name of the accused in the FIR is still listed as 'unknown.' The only reason Mahesh's name has surfaced is due to his association with Contractor Krishna, and that, Your Honor, is not enough to justify his arrest."

Shastry decided to address a point he knew the prosecution would bring up—that anticipatory bail should not be a shield for criminals.

"Your Lordship, I understand the concern of the prosecution, and I acknowledge that anticipatory bail is not intended to provide blanket immunity to anyone accused of a crime. The Supreme Court has repeatedly emphasized this in several judgments, including State of Bihar vs. Jang Bahadur, where it held that bail should not be granted as a matter of course. But, Your Honor, this case is not one where my client seeks to avoid justice; rather, he seeks to face it without the looming fear of arrest. He is prepared to cooperate fully with the investigation."

Shastry could feel the weight of his arguments settling into the room. Judge Shankar's expression remained neutral, but Shastry knew the judge was absorbing every word. Shastry paused for a moment, referring to his notes, before delivering his final points. The courtroom was utterly silent, everyone hanging on his next words.

"In conclusion, Your Honor, the anticipatory bail provision exists to ensure that no individual is unjustly deprived of their liberty. It is a means to protect personal freedom in a democratic society. The Supreme Court has clearly laid down that unless there are compelling reasons—like the potential to flee, tampers with evidence, or intimidate witnesses—anticipatory bail should be granted. My client, Mahesh, does not pose any such risk. He is a young man with no prior criminal record, and he seeks this Hon'ble Court's protection so that he may clear his name in a fair and just manner."

"Your Honor, my client is willing to comply with all conditions imposed by the court including furnishing necessary surety. He is not a flight risk, he has no prior criminal record, and he has already expressed his willingness to cooperate with the investigation. I respectfully submit that Mahesh should be granted anticipatory bail so that he can face the law with dignity, not as a fugitive but as a young man who seeks to clear his name from an alleged crime that he did not commit."

With that, Shastry stepped back from the podium, giving a slight nod of respect to Judge Shankar. Shastry had presented his case well, and the tension in the room was palpable as Shastry took his seat, the weight of the Supreme Court's principles still hanging in the air. Shastry had laid the foundation—a foundation built on landmark judgments, the sacred provision of personal liberty, and the very essence of justice. The courtroom remained silent for a few seconds as Judge Shankar leaned forward, deep in thought.

"Mr. Shastry, your arguments are well-placed," the judge finally said; his tone thoughtful. "I will consider them." "Post the case for orders tomorrow" "Adjourned!"

The next morning, Court Hall No. 67 was filled with a quiet buzz of anticipation. Lawyers, litigants, and clerks shuffled about, exchanging whispered conversations, while a few junior lawyers clutched their briefs, anxiously waiting for their cases to be called.

For Ramachandra Shastry, today was a big day. After weeks of intense preparation, late nights poring over caselaws, and hours spent fine-tuning his arguments, it had come down to this—the judgment on Criminal Miscellaneous Petition No. 3121/2010. This was Mahesh's future hanging in the balance.

The previous day's proceedings had ended with Public Prosecutor Himanand Kumar finishing his response, but the court had adjourned for the day, leaving both sides in a state of anxious suspense. Judge Shankar had reserved his order, promising to deliver it today.

As Shastry entered the court hall, he noticed a familiar sense of nervous energy in the air. Shastry made his way to the front of the courtroom, where Himanand Kumar was already seated. The prosecutor was flipping through his notes with an air of confidence, but even he seemed to acknowledge the weight of the moment. After all, they were both professionals, and they both knew this case could swing either way.

The room fell silent as the bench clerk stood up, his voice ringing through the hall.

"Silence!"

The heavy doors creaked open, and Judge Sri. Shankar entered, his robes swaying with a quiet authority. He walked briskly to his seat, adjusting his spectacles as he scanned the room before sitting down.

"Please be seated."

Everyone in the room sat, the air still charged with tension.

Judge Shankar adjusted the papers before him, flipping through the pages of his well-drafted order. Shastry could see the thick document in the judge's hands, and he felt a quiet satisfaction wash over him—this was going to be a detailed ruling.

"I have before me, the matter concerning the anticipatory bail application filed by the petitioner, Mahesh, under Section 438 of the Criminal Procedure Code for the offences punishable under sections 143, 147, 148, 448, 427, 307 and 149 of the Indian Penal Code, 1860." Judge Shankar's voice was calm, measured, and precise. "The prosecution has raised several objections to this application, while the defense has presented substantial grounds in favor of the bail. It is now my duty to address these issues in detail and render my judgment accordingly."

Shankar paused for a moment, glancing up at both Shastry and Himanand before continuing.

"The facts of the case are as follows: the petitioner, Mahesh, has been implicated in a matter involving his association with Contractor Krishna, who is accused of grievous assault. The prosecution's main contention is that Mahesh, although not named in the initial FIR, is allegedly involved in the criminal conspiracy."

Judge Shankar looked over at Himanand Kumar, his expression serious. "The prosecution, represented by Mr. Himanand Kumar, has objected to the grant of anticipatory bail on four primary grounds."

He read from his order.

"Firstly, the prosecution has argued that the petitioner is a flight risk, based on his association with known criminals. Secondly, it was suggested that Mahesh has been involved in other offenses, although no formal complaints have been lodged. Thirdly, the prosecution contends that Mahesh is not as innocent as portrayed by the defense, and finally, it is argued that keeping the petitioner in custody would allow him the opportunity to reform."

Shankar paused, his gaze sweeping the room as the weight of the objections settled over the audience.

"These objections have been noted carefully, and I shall address each one in turn."

Shastry felt a flicker of nerves as the judge continued.

"On the first objection, regarding Mahesh being a flight risk, this court finds that there is insufficient evidence to substantiate this claim. There has been no attempt by the petitioner to flee the jurisdiction, and the mere association with Contractor Krishna is not enough to assume that Mahesh would abscond if granted bail. This argument is speculative at best."

Shankar's words felt like small victories for Shastry, who kept his face neutral, but inside, he was beginning to feel hopeful.

"Secondly, the prosecution has mentioned that Mahesh may have been involved in other offenses, but again, no formal complaints or FIRs have been registered. It is the view of this court that justice cannot be served based on unverified rumors or fears. Without concrete evidence, this argument does not hold weight."

Shastry noticed Himanand Kumar shifting in his seat, clearly aware that his objections were being methodically dismantled.

"The third ground, that Mahesh is not innocent, is something this court views with caution. The presumption of innocence is a fundamental principle in our legal system, and until proven otherwise, the petitioner cannot be deemed guilty by association alone. The prosecution has not provided any direct evidence linking Mahesh to the assault in question."

There was a subtle but palpable change in the courtroom. Even Mahesh, sitting quietly beside his father, seemed to relax ever so slightly.

"In considering the petitioner's plea for anticipatory bail, this court is mindful of the principle of parity, which has been enshrined in numerous judicial pronouncements by the Hon'ble Supreme Court of India. It is essential that justice be applied equitably to all accused in a case unless there are compelling reasons to differentiate between them. In the present case, two co-accused, who were directly involved in the alleged offense, have already been granted bail by this court. The petitioner, Mahesh, is alleged to have played a far lesser role, with no direct evidence implicating him in the crime. In the absence of any distinguishing factors that would warrant a deviation from this principle, Mahesh is entitled to the same relief."

"Lastly, the argument that the petitioner's incarceration would serve as an opportunity for reform is, while well-intentioned, not a sufficient reason to deny bail. The purpose of bail is not to punish the accused before conviction but to ensure that they face trial fairly. Mahesh's time in custody, if any, should not be used as a tool for reform when the court has not yet determined his guilt."

Shastry felt his heart race as Judge Shankar turned his attention to the defense's case.

"Mr. Ramachandra Shastry, appearing for the petitioner, has presented his case with clarity and precision, citing numerous landmark judgments that guide this court in its decision." Shankar adjusted his glasses, clearly impressed. "Mr. Shastry has brought to the court's attention the celebrated judgment in Gurbaksh Singh Sibbia vs. State of Punjab, where the Supreme Court established that anticipatory bail is a tool to protect personal liberty and should not be denied merely because the accused is involved in a serious offense."

The room was silent as Shankar continued, his tone measured but filled with respect.

"In addition, Mr. Shastry has rightly relied on Siddharam Satlingappa Mhetre vs. State of Maharashtra, where the Supreme Court held that the personal liberty of an individual is one of the most cherished rights under the Constitution. This court finds that the principles laiddown in Mhetre apply directly to the present case."

Shastry could feel the praise settling over him like a mantle, and he remained composed, though inside, asmall part of him swelled with pride.

"The defense's submission that Mahesh's identity in the FIR is in question and that no overt acts have been attributed to him is a valid and persuasive argument. The defense has also highlighted the principle of parity, noting that two other accused in the same case have already been enlarged on bail. On this basis, Mahesh is also entitled to the same relief."

Judge Shankar flipped to the final page of his order and added, "Before I conclude, this court wishes to place on record a special appreciation for Mr. Ramachandra Shastry for his well-researched and insightful submissions. His arguments have not only illuminated the finer nuances of anticipatory bail but have also highlighted the importance of protecting individual liberty in our legal system."

Finally, Judge Shankar leaned back slightly, his gaze sweeping the courtroom before he delivered the final portion of his order.

"In view of the above, and taking into account the lack of concrete evidence against the petitioner, as well as the legal principles cited by the defense, this court is of the opinion that anticipatory bail should be granted to Mahesh."

Shankar's voice was calm, but his words carried the weight of finality.

"The petitioner, Mahesh, is granted anticipatory bail under Section 438 of Cr.P.C. on the following conditions:"

- Mahesh shall cooperate fully with the ongoing investigation and shall appear before the Investigating Officer within 15 days from the date of this order.
- He shall not leave the jurisdiction of the court without prior permission.
- He shall not tamper with any evidence or intimidate any witnesses.
- He shall furnish a surety bond of Rs.50,000.00

Shastry felt a small smile tug at his lips, but he kept his composure, simply bowing slightly in respect. He could feel a wave of relief wash over him. The victory was palpable, not just for him but for Mahesh, who had been living under the shadow of fear.

The judgment had been delivered. Mahesh would not have to fear the dark shadow of arrest any longer. The courtroom slowly began to clear, with people filing out, discussing the day's events.

As Shastry packed his papers into his bag, he felt a tap on his shoulder. He turned to see Nair standing there, his eyes filled with gratitude.

"Thank you, sir. Thank you for everything. You've given my son his life back."

Shastry nodded, placing a reassuring hand on Nair's shoulder. "This is just the beginning. We still have a long way to go, but for now, Mahesh is safe."

THE STORM IS COMING

The air in the police station was thick with tension. Ramachandra Shastry, dressed in a crisp white shirt and dark trousers, stood tall amidst the dim glow of incandescent bulbs. His face was calm, composed, but there was a sharpness in his eyes—an alertness that came from years of navigating murky legal waters. Across from him, Inspector Sridhar sat behind his cluttered desk, flipping through a pile of papers with deliberate slowness, a mocking smirk creeping onto his face.

Beside Shastry stood Mahesh, a young man, barely nineteen, trembling from head to toe. Mahesh's face was pale, his eyes wide with fear, his lips quivering as if wordscould escape at any moment. His innocence was as apparent as his terror. Accused of a crime he didn't commit—attempted murder under Section 307 of the Indian Penal Code—he had found solace only in Shastry's unwavering belief in his innocence.

Shastry held out a court order, his voice steady and measured. "Inspector Sridhar, as per the court's directive, I've brought Mahesh here within the stipulated fifteen days. The formalities should be complete."

Sridhar's gaze, dark and heavy with disdain, slowly lifted from the papers. His lips curled into a thin smile, more a sneer than a greeting. "So, this is the famous Ramachandra Shastry I keep hearing about, eh? And you've already gotten this boy—a murderer in the making—out on bail?"

Shastry's tone didn't falter. "He's not a murderer, Inspector. He's just a boy—nineteen years old. You know as well as I do that the charges were exaggerated. The injuries in the case don't even support an attempt to murder."

Sridhar leaned back in his chair, fingers tapping the wooden armrests as though contemplating some private joke. His eyes glinted with malice. "Exaggerated, you say? We'll see about that."

The inspector stood up, his movements slow and deliberate, like a predator about to spring. From a drawer, he pulled out a file and slammed it onto the table. The noise echoed in the small room. He flipped through the pages before pulling out a fresh document and handing it to Shastry.

Mocking laughter laced Sridhar's voice. "While you were busy playing the hero in court, I was doing my job. Surprises come easy in my line of work, Mr. Shastry. Your innocent boy here isn't just facing attempted murder anymore. We've got something bigger now."

With a theatrical flourish, Sridhar pulled out an arrest warrant, slamming it down on the table. The sound reverberated through the room like a thunderclap.

"Say hello to your client's new charges: preparation to commit Dacoity! Section 399 and 402 of the IPC. And guess what? He's not going anywhere."

Shastry's calm façade wavered for a split second as he scanned the new document. His sharp eyes widened ever so slightly, a flicker of shock that he quickly masked. But Mahesh wasn't as composed. The boy's knees buckled, his breath quickening, beads of sweat trickling down his forehead.

"Sir... I didn't... I wasn't involved in anything like that," Mahesh stammered, his voice barely above a whisper, desperation seeping into every word. Shastry straightened; his resolve hardening. He had been in situations like this before—facing off against police officers who wielded their power like weapons, bending the law to their will.

"Inspector, this is absurd. You know Mahesh had nothing to do with any dacoity. You're using this as a pretext, just because I got him bail. I urge you—don't ruin this young man's life with a false charge."

Sridhar's grin widened, cold and cruel. "Don't lecture me, Shastry. You're a lawyer, I'm a police officer. You do your work, I'll do mine."

At his signal, a constable stepped forward, handcuffs in hand. Mahesh's eyes filled with terror as the cold steel locked around his wrists, the finality of it crashing over him like a tidal wave. Shastry's jaw clenched, his fists curling tightly by his sides.

"Inspector, I've always respected the law, and so should you. You know this is wrong. He's just a boy—don't destroy his future over a personal grudge against me," Shastry said, his voice calm but edged with steel. Sridhar's eyes narrowed, his voice dropping to a low, menacing tone. "This is my station, Shastry. You may win in court, but out here, it's my rules. Don't forget that."

As the constables led a tearful Mahesh away, Shastry remained still, watching the boy's retreating figure. His heart pounded with a mixture of anger and resolve, but outwardly, he was calm, his face a mask of stoic determination. Sridhar turned his back, dismissing him with a wave of his hand. "Now get out of here. We'll see how long your clever arguments can keep him safe."

Shastry didn't respond. He knew the battle had just begun. As he stepped out of the station into the cold night air, the weight of what was to come pressed down on him. The storm was coming, and Ramachandra Shastry was ready to face it head-on.

For justice wasn't just a profession for him—it was a calling. Nair, Mahesh's father was shocked at the events taking place before his eyes and in his heart, he knew that no matter how dark the path became, Shastry would fight to his last breath to ensure that the truth prevailed.

UNPACKING THE LAW

Back in his office, Shastry's bookshelf stood like a silent testament to his commitment to the law, though it was anything but grand. He took a seat at his desk, casting a glance at the modest collection of books that had become his lifeline. Despite his lean library, each book was an anchor in his practice. On one end of the shelf sat a faded red copy of the Criminal Manual—a gift from an enthusiastic candidate who once sought his help in a local Bar association election. Next to it were his well-thumbed copies of the Constitution, Indian Penal Code (IPC), Criminal Procedure Code (Cr.P.C.), and the Indian Evidence Act, all bare acts he'd received over the years, their pages softened by countless flips and marked by notes scribbled in the margins.

Every now and then, when a particularly stubborn provision or an unusual case came his way, Shastry would turn to his battered commentary volumes: Ratanlal & Dhirajlal on the IPC and Cr.P.C., along with textbooks from his law school days—remnants of a time when the theoretical world of law was full of idealistic promise.

But there was a hitch. His greatest frustration was his lack of access to law journals. He often found himself trekking to the High Court or Civil Court library, spending hours sifting through dusty shelves for a citation, only to come up empty-handed.

With a sigh, he remembered previous instances of wild goose chase for Supreme Court judgments, which often turned out to be a misquote after hours of scouring. Returning his focus to the task at hand, he picked up Ratanlal & Dhirajlal on the IPC and flipped it open to Section 399, skimming through the carefully highlighted lines that detailed the provision of preparation to commit dacoity.

Section 399, he read silently, deals with "preparation to commit dacoity." It was a provision not often charged, but one that held a particular weight when invoked. It essentially criminalized the preparation stage of dacoity—when a group, with intent and some level of planning, had begun to gear up for a dacoity without necessarily executing it yet. Shastry smirked at the phrase "preparation to commit," knowing that, legally, this word "preparation" was key. It was the only provision in the entire Indian Penal Code, 1860 where the "PREPARATION" to commit itself amounted to Actus Reus.

Flipping a page, he noted that Section 399 required two main elements: (1) intent to commit dacoity and (2) preparation to act on that intent. If Mahesh were arrested for his connection to a gang planning dacoity, the law stipulated that the prosecution would need to demonstrate a "specific preparation" linked to a particular target. Mere association wasn't enough; they had to prove his actions indicated that he was ready to move beyond thought to physical action.

The next provision, Section 402, caught his eye and he gave it a thorough read. This one criminalized the assembly of persons for the purpose of committing dacoity. For this, a meeting or gathering was needed, where the purpose of that gathering was clear. It was broader than Section 399 but equally severe—essentially treating a group of people who merely gathered to plan a dacoity with almost the same scrutiny as if they had actually committed it. He sighed, closing the book momentarily, deep in thought. Tapping the cover of the book, he muttered "if only this was as clear-cut as it sounds. One vague step and its back to the Civil Court library for hours."

Next Day, with a renewed sense of focus, Shastry went to the Magistrate Court complex and applied and took all the certified copies of FIR pertaining to the new case hoisted on Mahesh and returned back to his office to draft the bail application.

The facts of the case as prepared and presented by Inspector Sridhar in the First Information Report were that he received information from his informant on 04/01/2011 at around 10:45 p.m. that, a group of people had gathered in order to commit a crime near 4th 'N' Block. He has further alleged that he had received information that the people who had gathered were in possession of dangerous weapons and were deliberating upon a plan in order to commit an offence and that he along with his staff and colleagues secretly hid behind a tree and overheard the conversation of the gang of accused persons and heard that they were deliberating a plan as to commit dacoity by snatching gold ornaments from the people who werewalking by.

That after confirming that the Accused persons had in-fact gathered to commit dacoity, he asked the Panchayathdars to come to the alleged place and along-with a few constables attacked at once and caught hold of four people and the remaining two persons escaped in the dark. He further went on alleging that he in the presence of the Panchayathdars started frisking and recovered a chilli powder packet, a wooden stick, and a small knife and arrested those four people for offences under sections 399, 400 IPC in Crime No. 005/2011. Mahesh's name was not even mentioned in the FIR! He was now being arrayed as an accused in the place of "2 unknown persons".

Shastry shifted his focus on the remand application which pertained to Mahesh. A remand application is a legal request that police or investigating authorities submit to the court, seeking permission to keep a person in custody for further investigation. It also explains how, when and where was the Accused person arrested. It was a fabricated story created in the Mahesh's remand application that he was arrested at a bus stop nearby while trying to leave the city.

Shastry glanced at the clock, realizing he'd been lost in his thoughts for over an hour. He stood up, stretched, and reached for his pocket and lit a cigarette.

After hours of reading, Shastry leaned back and reflected on what he'd learned. He mused over how he'd explain Sections 399 and 402 in the simplest terms before the jduge. He decided that Section 399 was like catching someone just before the robbery—if they were gathering weapons, planning the route, or discussing escape, that was a punishable "preparation."

And Section 402? Well, that was like penalizing a team huddle, where everyone involved was planning the crime, even if they hadn't yet acted. As he looked at the bare acts lined up on his desk, he could almost see the laws as characters—each with its own quirks, its own pitfalls, and, at times, its stubborn resistance to being pinned down. These laws were both rigid and elusive, their interpretation so critical to the course of justice.

After hours at the desk, Shastry's stomach grumbled, interrupting his train of thought. He grabbed a chocolate cream bun bought from Ramesh's shop for lunch. "Lawyer's life!" he chuckled, biting into it, crumbs scattering over his commentary. "I'd be better off if Ratanlal & Dhirajlal included a section on survival tactics for underpaid lawyers."

A knock on the door brought him out of his reverie, and he opened it to see Ramesh, the shopkeeper with a glass of coffee. "Saar, when people like you work so hard, even the law gods must listen. Take a break! A lot can happen over a coffee! He winked!" Taking a sip of the coffee, Shastry let the warmth seep through him, grateful for the small comforts.

Back to work, refocused, Shastry turned back to his desk, he started to draft the bail application. As the evening wore on, his office fell silent, and under the dim light, Shastry's keyboard continued its journey crafting the defense that would soon face the full might of the courtroom.

The next morning, Shastry arrived at the courthouse early, his backpack swinging at his side with every determined step. As he entered the court hall, the atmosphere was electric. Lawyers whispered in corners, litigantsanxiously clutched their files, and court staff moved briskly through the crowd. Shastry could feel the tension in the air—a combination of anticipation and curiosity. Shastry scanned the room as he took his seat.

His case, Criminal Miscellaneous Petition No.:8456/10, was slotted at No. 14 in the list. His mind raced through his prepared arguments: the travesty of justice, Inspector Sridhar had committed; the violation of Mahesh's rights, and the high-handed manner in which the law had been twisted. He knew he could make a strong case for Mahesh, a young man swept up into a world he didn't deserve.

Finally, when his case was called, he rose, ready to command the court's attention. But before he could say a word, Judge Sudhakar Shetty glanced over at the Public Prosecutor and spoke in a clear, unwavering voice.

"PP!," Judge Shetty began, his tone assertive but calm, "all the other individuals arrested in this case were granted bail just two days ago. In light of this, I am inclined to grant similar orders in the case of this petitioner also." He paused, allowing his words to sink in. "Please file any objections by the end of business today, and I will post this matter for orders tomorrow."

Shastry was taken aback. The judge's words washed over him like a tide of relief, even before he had argued a single point. He stood there, momentarily speechless, as Judge Shetty's firm tone had already addressed the critical arguments he had prepared.

Gathering himself, Shastry began, "Thank you, Your Honor. If I may add—"

Judge Shetty raised a hand, signaling for him to pause. "Mr. Shastry, I understand the points you want to make, but I am already inclined towards granting bail, with necessary conditions. There's no need to further elaborate today. The order will be passed tomorrow."

Relief flooded through Shastry's veins, though he felt a surge of pride as well. Judge Shetty's decision affirmed everything he believed about justice and truth. As he stepped back from the podium, he caught sight of Nair seated in the back row. The older man's eyes sparkled with hope, and the two shared a brief but meaningful nod.

As Shastry and Nair left the court hall, Nair could hardly contain his joy. "Sir, this is beyond anything we had hoped for! You are... you are a godsend, truly!"

Shastry chuckled. "Hold your gratitude until Mahesh is out, Nair. Remember, this is just one battle, but tomorrow, I believe, we'll see the beginning of Mahesh's new life."

Nair nodded fervently. "You have no idea what this means to us, Shastry Sir. I've spent sleepless nights worrying about Mahesh, and knowing that you're by our side—" Shastry placed a comforting hand on Nair's shoulder. "He deserves a chance, and it's my job to see that he gets it. Justice doesn't rest, and neither will I."

When Shastry returned to his office, he noticed an imposing black Mercedes-Benz parked outside. Four well-dressed men stepped out as he approached, their appearance professional yet discreet. One of them stepped forward and greeted Shastry with a polite nod.

"Mr. Shastry, my name is Gangadhar," he introduced himself with a gentle smile. "I believe my car service station recently had the pleasure of availing your legal services."

Shastry looked surprised but extended his hand warmly. "Ah, yes, Mr. Gangadhar. I didn't realize you'd want to meet me in person."

Gangadhar nodded, a humble tone in his voice. "I've heard quite a bit about your efforts to help our young employee, Gopala. I was abroad during the entire situation, but upon learning about what you did—not only for him but also for the way it united the employees—I felt compelled to come and meet you personally."

Shastry led him into his modest office, gesturing for him to take a seat. He cleared a stack of books from one chair and offered it to Gangadhar, who took it without hesitation.

"Mr. Shastry, from now on, I would like you to be our company's legal counsel. Your sense of justice and the empathy you showed towards Gopala… it's rare. Truly."

Shastry tried to brush it off modestly, but Gangadhar continued, "In my line of work, I've come across many lawyers, but I've seldom seen anyone balance their profession with such compassion. So, as of today, you are officially our retained counsel."

Shastry's eyes lit up. He shook Gangadhar's hand, feeling a rush of gratitude. "Thank you, Mr. Gangadhar," he said sincerely. "I'll do my best."

Gangadhar smiled. "I don't doubt it. And please, if you ever need anything—resources, connections, even support for your cases—consider me a friend. Don't hesitate to ask."

As Shastry absorbed Gangadhar's words, he felt a spark. "Actually, there's something you could do… for someone else."

Gangadhar's eyebrows rose with interest. "Of course. Tell me."

Shastry leaned forward, his voice sincere. "There's a young boy named Mahesh. He's been through a lot and was caught up in the wrong crowd. I believe he's a good soul at heart, just needs the right opportunity. Once he's out on bail, he'll need a fresh start. Perhaps… a job at your service station?"

Gangadhar didn't hesitate. "Consider it done. Themoment he's out, have him report to my team. I'll see that he's given a fair chance."

Shastry's relief was evident. "Thank you, Mr. Gangadhar. You may have just changed his life."

Gangadhar placed a reassuring hand on Shastry's shoulder. "No, Mr. Shastry. It's you who changed his life. I'm merely following your lead."

That evening, Shastry called Nair to give him the good news. "Nair, I have a place for Mahesh once he's out. A steady job at Gangadhar's service station as a mechanic."

There was a stunned silence on the other end of the line before Nair's choked voice came through. "Shastry Sir... I don't have words. You have... you have done what a father couldn't. I don't know how to repay you."

"There's no need for repayment, Nair," Shastry replied warmly. "This is just one step in the right direction. Mahesh deserves a future, and now he'll have one. When he's released, take him straight to Gangadhar's place, and from there, let him start anew."

Nair's voice trembled with emotion. "Sir, you're wise beyond your years. You're more than a lawyer—you're a blessing to people like us." Shastry smiled to himself, the weight of the day's events settling over him. He leaned back in his chair, feeling both a sense of accomplishment and a profound gratitude.

"Thank you, Nair," he said finally. "Remember, justice doesn't always come from the law alone. Sometimes, it's about doing what's right, even if it's outside the court's walls."

That night, Shastry sat in his quiet office, reflecting on the events of the past weeks—the battles fought, the victories won, and the lives changed. The journey had been long and arduous, but as he looked at the growing stack of cases on his desk, he knew his work had only just begun. Justice, he realized, wasn't merely about statutes and provisions; it was about the heart and the resolve to make things right, one case at a time.

UNDER THE JULY SKY- 2011

The morning sun peeked through the slats of Shastry's modest office window, casting a soft glow on his newly acquired pride and joy: a sleek, black Dell laptop, resting on his desk like a crown jewel. Its glossy finish reflected the beams of light, and Shastry couldn't resist running his fingers over the brand logo one more time. The laptop had been a dream for so long—a quiet symbol of progress and persistence—and here it was, finally within his reach.

With a satisfied smile, he glanced over to the side where his brand-new HP laser printer stood proudly. It was a significant upgrade from the outdated, groaning relic he'd relied on for so long. This machine purred with every page, its efficiency almost startling after years of coaxing his old printer to life with gentle taps and whispered threats. As it printed out a crisp, clean document, Shastry leaned back in his chair, savoring the ease of this newfound simplicity.

The faint aroma of fresh paper and printer ink filled the room as he placed his hands on his laptop, opening it to reveal a crisp, high-resolution screen. Gone were the days of spending hours flipping through the dusty archives in court libraries. With a few keystrokes, Shastry had access to digital libraries, case laws, and the latest precedents from around the world. The convenience made him feel as if he'd stepped into the future—a lawyer on the cutting edge, equipped with every tool he needed.

As he typed, his fingers danced confidently over the keyboard, the letters of a new case coming to life on the screen. The steady income from the car service station retainer had done more than allow him these purchases; it had given him peace of mind, a steady rhythm to his life that extended beyond the walls of his small office.

And he wasn't the only one who noticed.

His usual morning routine of tea, biscuits, and conversation at Ramesh's shop had taken on a new tone. Where before, people might have seen a struggling young lawyer, they now saw a confident, reliable advocate.

Narayan the landlord came by, waving warmly, and Ramesh, who had once teased Shastry about his tattered practice and old equipment, now watched with admiration.

"New laptop, Shastry Sir?" Narayan called out as Shastry approached to hand over the monthly rent, his black Dell laptop safely stowed in his bag. Shastry nodded with a grin, placing his order. "Yes, sir. It's a small upgrade, but one that makes a world of difference."

"Ah, our Shastry Sir is moving up in the world!" Narayan clapped, nodding appreciatively. "First the printer, now a laptop. Soon, we'll see you in a big office in a fancy suit!"

Shastry laughed, "Let's not get ahead of ourselves sir. For now, I'm just glad to pay rent every month and have fewer trips to the library."

As he finished his conversation, Shastry felt a sense of calm he hadn't experienced before. His little office, with its new additions, was more than just a workspace now—it was a place of steady progress, a hub of justice in its own right. The foundation was set; he could feel it. And with every new case, with every client who walked through his door, Shastry's vision of making a difference grew sharper, stronger, more assured.

Six months had passed since Ramachandra Shastry had first walked out of Inspector Sridhar's police station, determined to fight for justice. The memory of that fateful day, when the system had almost swallowed young Mahesh whole, had fueled him to work harder and smarter. But success had not come without its costs. The road had been long, full of challenges, betrayals, and moments of doubt. His journey was far from over, but with each step, he could see the path unfolding, a bright road ahead for Lawyer Ramachandra Shastry.

DEBT REPAID!

Now, in a quiet corner of Bengaluru, the city's bustling chaos seemed to fade. The sun was setting over Cubbon Park, casting long shadows across the grass, as Chaya sat on a bench, her laughter ringing out. She was sitting beside Mahendra, who, in contrast to Shastry's life of legal battles, had an air of effortless charm. He was warm, witty, and seemed to bring light wherever he went. Today, they were sharing an ice cream, a moment of simplicity amidst the complexities of life.

Mahendra's eyes sparkled as he watched her laugh. "You know," he said, smiling, "I've never met anyone who makes me laugh as much as you do."

Chaya, blushing at the compliment, nudged him playfully. "Oh, stop it. You're just saying that."

But Mahendra's tone shifted, becoming soft, sincere. "No, really. You're like sunshine in human form." He paused, searching her face. "I'm really glad we met, Chaya. You've become important to me."

Chaya's laughter faded into a shy smile. She lookeddown, fiddling with the edge of her ice cream cup. "Me too," she whispered.

For a moment, the world stood still around them. Mahendra took her hand, his touch warm and reassuring. "I want to be someone you can trust," he said, his voice barely above a whisper. "You know that, right?"

Chaya looked up, her heart fluttering. "I do," she replied, her voice soft but certain. And in that moment, she believed him. His charm, his confidence, and the way he made her feel—everything seemed surreal.

Yet, beneath the surface of their growing romance, something darker was brewing.

Weeks passed, and Chaya's feelings for Mahendra deepened. They talked every day, late into the night, their conversations filled with laughter, dreams, and promises. Mahendra had become a constant in her life, and she found herself falling for him in ways she hadn't expected.

But as their relationship grew closer, so did Mahendra's ambitions. One evening, while sitting in her family's living room, Mahendra presented Chaya with an opportunity—a government project, an investment that could set her up for life. All it needed was an initial investment of Rupees 10 lakhs.

Chaya hesitated. "Ten lakh is a lot of money, Mahendra. It's my family's savings," she said, her voice tinged with doubt.

But Mahendra leaned closer, his voice smooth and persuasive. "I get that, Chaya. But trust me; I wouldn't bring this to you if I wasn't sure about it. I want to build a future with you." His eyes softened as he added, "You trust me, don't you?"

Chaya's heart raced. She did trust him, didn't she? Mahendra had been nothing but kind and supportive. Slowly, she nodded. "I trust you," she whispered. That decision would mark the beginning of a nightmare she never saw coming.

Days turned into weeks, and the silence from Mahendra grew deafening. Chaya's phone calls went unanswered, her messages ignored. She sat by her phone, anxiety gnawing at her as each day passed without word from him.

"Mahendra, it's me again," Chaya left another voicemail, her voice trembling. "I'm just calling to see if there's any update on the project. Please call me back when you get this."

Her heart sank as she hung up. Something wasn't right. The man who had once filled her world with warmth and light was now a shadow, slipping further away from her reach.

Her brother, Kiran Kumar, noticed the change. He found her sitting alone one evening, her face pale with worry. "Chaya," he said gently, sitting beside her. "What's going on? You've been acting strange for days."

Chaya hesitated, her voice catching in her throat. "I've made a huge mistake, Kumar. I trusted the wrong person." She swallowed hard, fighting back tears. "Mahendra... he tricked me. I gave him Rupees 10 lakh for a project, but now he's disappeared. He won't give it back. He's even threatened me."

Kiran's face darkened with fury. "What?! That son of Manjunatha Gowda? I knew something was off about him!"

Chaya's tears flowed freely now, her body trembling. "I don't know what to do, Kumar. I feel so helpless." Kumar clenched his fists. "Don't worry, Chaya. I'll make him pay for this. No one cheats my sister and gets away with it."

The next night, Kumar gathered his closest friends—Prasad, Raghu, Partha, Krishna, and Ahmed—in a small, dimly lit room. The tension was palpable as they discussed what had happened.

"Mahendra tricked my sister. Rs. 10 lakh gone, just like that. And now he's threatening her!" Kumar's voice was cold with rage. Prasad slammed his fist on the table. "That scumbag! We can't let him get away with this." Raghu nodded in agreement. "What's the plan, Kumar?" "We're going to his shop tomorrow," Kumar said, his eyes flashing with anger. "He thinks he can hide behind his family's business, but we'll make sure he knows what it feels like to mess with us."

Ahmed, always the cautious one, spoke up. "Are you sure about this, Kiran? We could get into serious trouble." Kumar's expression was hard. "This isn't just about money. It's about Chaya's dignity. We'll go, show him we mean business, but we're not going to do anything reckless. Just scare him enough to return the money." Partha grinned, a glint of mischief in his eyes. "Count me in. I've got a few tricks to scare him good."

And so, the wheels of revenge were set in motion as they prepared for the confrontation that would come, none of them knew that this would only be the beginning of a much larger storm—a storm that would sweep through their lives, bringing them face to face with justice, betrayal, and the true cost of trust.

The next day, early afternoon when the sun was blazing outside, the mobile phone repair shop in North Bengaluru was filled with customers, and the soft hum of electronics buzzing around. Phones are ringing, people were chatting, and the sound of keyboard's clicking filled the air, Manjunatha Gowda, an elderly man in his 60s, was seated behind the counter, his back slightly hunched from years of hard work. He wiped his brow with a handkerchief as he fixed a phone under a magnifying glass. His movements were steady but slow, reflecting his age.

Suddenly, the glass door to the shop swung open violently, causing the small bell at the top to jangle furiously. Kiran Kumar stormed in, followed by Prasad, Raghu, Partha, Krishna, and Ahmed. The air shifted with their presence. Customers glanced nervously, sensing the tension. "Manjunatha Gowda! You think your son can cheat my sister and get away with it?" Kumar screamed loudly and menacingly. Manjunatha Gowda nervously put the phone down and stood up startled, trying to stay calm.

But before he could say a word, Kumar slammed his fist onto the counter, rattling the glass display case. The customers froze, watching the scenes unfold, but no one dared to intervene. One by one, the customers left the small shop.

"You owe us for what your son did" growled Prasad. Manjunatha Gowda tried to plead and raised his hands, signaling to calm them. Suddenly, Raghu grabbed a nearby display phone and hurled it against the wall. The sound of shattering glass echoed through the shop. Krishna and Ahmed began sweeping phones off the shelves with aggressive swipes, the sound of plastic and metal clattering to the floor. Manjunatha Gowda watched helplessly as his shop was being torn apart before his eyes.

Manjunatha Gowda stepped toward Kumar, but Partha, standing behind him, shoved him hard. Gowda stumbled forward and crashed into the counter, groaning as he fell to the ground. His head hit the corner of the wooden counter, and he winced, blood slowly trickling down his forehead.

Kumar, seething with anger, grabbed a metal rod lying on the side and moves toward Gowda, his eyes burning with rage. "You'll pay for your son's mistakes!" Kumar fumed. Without hesitation, Kumar brought the rod down, aiming for Manjunatha's side. The old man raised his arm to block the blow, but the impact cracked against his forearm, sending a wave of searing pain through his body. He let out a cry of agony, cradling his injured arm as he writhed on the floor.

The other gang members continued their rampage. Prasad kicked over a display case, the glass shattering and scattering across the floor like a glittering sea of shards. Raghu punched the lights, plunging part of the shop into flickering darkness.

From outside, a passerby caught sight of the chaos through the window and shouted alarmingly. "Someone call the police! Hurry!" The commotion began to draw crowd. Other shopkeepers peered out from their stores, their eyes wide with shock. Some pulled out their phones to record the scene; others ran to call for help. Inside the shop, the gang started to panic, realizing that attention is building outside.

"We need to get out of here urgently, Kumar!" Ahmed gasped! Kumar, breathing heavily, stood over Manjunatha Gowda, the rod still clenched in his hand. Gowda was barely able to move, tried to push himself up from the floor, his face was pale with pain. Blood from his forehead pooled on the floor, mixing with the shattered glass. "This isn't over." Kumar sneered. He tossed the rod aside, its metallic clang against the ground echoing ominously as the gang made a run for the door. They shove past the crowd gathering outside and disappeared into the narrow lanes behind the market.

As they fled, Gowda was left lying on the floor, gasping for breath, his body aching and his shop in ruins. Neighbors rushed in, kneeling beside him, their faces filled with concern. "He's hurt badly! Someone please get an ambulance!" a neighbor shouted. Manjunatha Gowda's eyes fluttered as he struggled to stay conscious. The last thing he heard was the sound of sirens wailing in the distance before everything went black.

The narrow, bustling streets of North Bengaluru were quieter than usual. Late in the evening, the clamor of auto rickshaws and street vendors had died down, leaving only the hum of distant traffic. Inside a small tea stall tucked in the shadows, Kiran Kumar sat at a corner table with his gang—Prasad, Raghu, Partha, Krishna, and Ahmed. The air was thick with tension, though no one spoke of it. They thought they were safe. They thought they were invisible.

Kumar sipped his tea, his eyes flicking between his friends. Prasad nervously drummed his fingers on the wooden table, while Partha stole glances at the entrance, his foot tapping impatiently. Raghu and Ahmed tried to look casual, leaning back in their chairs, but the unease in their posture betrayed their attempts.

Kumar leaned forward, his voice barely above a whisper. "We just need to lay low for a few more days. The police have bigger problems to deal with. No one's going to bother with us over an old man and his shop."

Prasad shifted in his seat, wiping his sweaty palms on his jeans. "I don't know, Kumar. Feels like something's off. Too many cops around these days." Kumar scoffed, though his own eyes darted toward the door. "Relax. We didn't leave any evidence. No cameras, no witnesses. Besides, it's not like they've got us on tape or anything." But Kumar was wrong.

Inspector Sridhar stood with his hands clasped behind his back in the police control room, his gaze fixed on the live feed from a public CCTV camera positioned outside the tea stall where Kumar and his gang were sitting. Sridhar's expression was calm, calculated, a man in complete control of the situation. His officers, dressed in plainclothes, were stationed strategically around the area, waiting for the signal to strike. Sridhar tapped his fingers on the desk, listening to the chatter of his team through his earpiece. He lifted his radio, his voice firm but steady.

"We've got eyes on them. I want this clean—no slip-ups. We take them all at once. They think they're safe in the shadows, but they're about to learn otherwise."

Outside, the police jeeps were parked in alleyways, hidden from view but ready to pounce. Officers checked their weapons, radios crackling softly as they awaited the order. Sridhar's gaze never wavered from the screen. He could feel the tension in the air, the calm before the storm.

"Go," he said quietly. "Now."

The sound of distant engines suddenly grew louder, disrupting the tense silence inside the stall. Prasad's eyes widened in panic as he glanced out the window. "Something's wrong." Before anyone could react, police jeeps screeched around the corner, blocking both ends of the narrow street. Doors swung open, and officers in plainclothes emerged from the shadows, moving with military precision. The tea stall, once a sanctuary, had become a trap. "It's the cops!" Ahmed's voice cracked with fear as he jumped to his feet, knocking over his cup of tea.

Before they could make sense of what was happening, the officers descended on them. One officer grabbed Kumar, slamming him onto the pavement with brutal force. Prasad tried to run, but another officer caught him, pinning him against the stall's counter.

Chaos erupted around them. The gang, stunned and disoriented, was no match for the swift precision of the police. Raghu and Partha were taken down before they could move, their faces pressed against the cold ground as handcuffs clicked into place as the gang was being bundled up to be brought to the police station.

"You're not as clever as you think, Kumar," Sub-Inspector Thimmaiah said, his voice laced with cold satisfaction. Kumar glared up at him, defiant even in his defeat. "You think this is over? It's not. We'll get out on bail, and when we do..." Thimmaiah cut him off, snapping handcuffs onto his wrists with a decisive click. "You won't get out as easily this time. Attempt to murder, robbery, assault, conspiracy whatnot? —you're going away for a long time." Kumar gritted his teeth, his chest heaving with anger. He knew the game was over, but his hatred burned brighter than ever.

Sridhar instructed on radio to his second-in-command, Officer Thimmaiah, who was coordinating the transport of the gang to the station. "Take them in," Sridhar said, his voice calm but authoritative. "I want full reports on my desk by tomorrow morning."

The officers nodded, shoving Kumar and his gang into the cell. Kumar and his gang were seated in a holding cell, bruised and disheartened. The tension was palpable as they waited for what's coming next.

"They think this is over. But I swear, when we get out of here, Mahendra will pay for what he's done" said Kumar gritting his teeth. Prasad leaned against the wall, defeated: "Kumar, do you really think we're getting out of this? Sridhar's got us for attempt to murder, vandalism, assault, and God knows what else."

We'll get bail. We've got connections. But when we do… we'll settle this once and for all" Kumar smirked, hiding his fear. Ahmed shifted nervously, with his hands trembling slightly. "We barely got out of that raid. What if Sridhar has more evidence? What if we're stuck here for months?" Ahmed worried.

"Enough with the what-ifs! We'll handle it. I'm not letting my sister's reputation or my family's pride be dragged through the dirt because of that scumbag." Kumar snarled.

Back in the quiet of the dimly lit dining room, the only sound was the faint clinking of Chaya's trembling spoon against the cup, the tea inside barely touched. Her mother sat beside her, gripping her hand in a gentle, grounding touch. The warmth of her mother's palm felt like the only thing anchoring her to reality in this whirlwind of betrayal and scandal.

Chaya's gaze drifted over to the framed photos on the wall, each snapshot capturing a happier time—a family holiday, her graduation, Kumar's beaming smile on his first day at his new job. Now, that same brother was behind bars, entangled in a situation he'd been pulled into because of her. The guilt twisted her insides like a knife.

Her mother's soft voice broke through her reverie.

"It's not your fault, Chaya. Kumar was only trying to protect you" said Chaya's Mother gently. Chaya blinked, her vision blurred with unshed tears. Her voice was a whisper, raw and edged with pain. "But this is all because of me, Amma. I trusted Mahendra, and now… now our family's name is being dragged through the mud. Kumar's in jail because of me" replied Chaya tearfully.

Her mother's expression softened, sadness mingling with an unspoken fierceness. She placed her other hand atop Chaya's, enveloping her daughter's trembling fingers with both hands.

Chaya closed her eyes, but the ache in her chest refused to yield. She'd heard rumors—whispers that Mahendra's family, influential and connected, had no intention of letting this incident stain their reputation. They had resources, allies, and a determination to quash anything that could tarnish their image. Chaya knew that her brother's release wouldn't be a matter of simply presenting the truth. No, this was far more complicated.

She opened her eyes, a spark of determination flickering within her as she met her mother's gaze.

"I've been hearing rumors, Amma. Mahendra's family isn't going to let this go easily. They'll use every connection, every ounce of influence they have to keep Kumar locked away and our family silenced. We need more than just a legal strategy... we need someone who understands what's at stake. Someone smart... someone relentless." Chaya's voice steadied and resolve hardened.

Her mother studied her face, seeing the change in her daughter's expression. Chaya was no longer the young woman devastated by betrayal—she was a sister on a mission, prepared to fight for her family's honor. This wasn't just about clearing Kumar's name; it was about protecting everything they held dear.

Her mother took a deep breath, her face lined with worry but also with trust. "I know someone who might help," she said softly. "You go and meet Sub-Inspector Thimmaiah. They say he's relentless, but he has a sense of fairness that's hard to find. He might refer to a lawyer who might help us."

Chaya nodded, the name settling into her mind. Thimmaiah. She would meet with him, tell him everything, and hope that he was exactly the ally she needed to set things right.

Chaya stepped into the police station, her heart pounding as she glanced around the dingy, chaotic room. Officers shuffled through stacks of paperwork, a few rough-looking men were huddled in a corner, and the faint smell of stale coffee hung in the air. She wasn't used to this world, yet here she was—an outsider, forced into itsmidst, compelled by desperation.

The man she was here to see, Sub-Inspector Thimmaiah, was finishing up with a case when he noticed her standing at the door, visibly uneasy. He gestured for her to take a seat opposite his cluttered desk.

As she settled in, Thimmaiah leaned forward, his face calm but alert. "You're Kumar's sister, right?" His voice was gentle, but his eyes were sharp. She nodded, feeling a lump in her throat.

"Tell me," He said, watching her intently.

Chaya took a deep breath, gathering her thoughts. She poured her heart out—how Mahendra, the man she'd once trusted, had led her family into this nightmare; how her brother had been drawn in, attempting to protect her, only to find himself caught up in false accusations and powerful enemies. She confessed her fears, her suspicions about Mahendra's influential family pulling strings behind the scenes, and the suffocating guilt she carried for Kumar's plight.

When she finished, there was a moment of silence. Sub-Inspector Thimmaiah leaned back in his chair, nodding slowly as he processed her words. Then, a slight smile crossed his face.

"Chaya," he began, his voice warm, "I know someone who might just be the ally you need right now. A lawyer who's a bit… unconventional, let's say. He's young but sharp—Ramachandra Shastry. In fact, he chuckled, "he's got quite a reputation in the legal circles around here for his knack in securing bails and a sharp sense for justice."

Chaya's eyes lit up, hope stirring for the first time in days. "Sir, do you really think he can help Kumar?"

Thimmaiah's gaze grew serious. "Look, I'll be honest with you. I've seen my fair share of lawyers, but Shastry... he's different. He doesn't just see a case file; he sees the people behind it. He doesn't care about status, doesn't bow to pressure. Once he's in, he's very determined and, sometimes, downright relentless." Thimmaiah grinned, shaking his head.

Chaya felt her heart flutter with a renewed sense of purpose, yet she needed more than assurances. "But... can he handle someone like Mahendra's family?"

"Ah, Mahendra's family might have money and connections," Thimmaiah said with a smirk, "but Shastry has something much better—an indomitable spirit. I remember one case... he fought tooth and nail for a young boy named Mahesh who was in deeper trouble than Kumar and his gang. Shastry stood his ground, unflinching. When he took that case, it was like watching a dog with a bone—he just wouldn't let go until justice was served."

He paused, his gaze softening. "He's a rare breed, Chaya. He fights hard for the underdog, for people who've been wronged, and he doesn't get intimidated. If you can tell him your story, and if he believes there's truth to it, I can guarantee he'll go to the ends of the earth to bring Kumar home."

Chaya felt tears prick her eyes. For the first time, she felt like she could see a way through this nightmare. "Thank you, Sub-Inspector Thimmaiah. I'll go to him ... I'll find Ramachandra Shastry and meet him in his office."

Thimmaiah reached across the table and gave her the contact number of Shastry. "Just remember, Chaya, you're not alone. There are people out here who'll fight for justice, and sometimes... you just need to find the right one and I believe Shastry is the one.

The day was turning darker as storm clouds gathered above Bengaluru, thick and brooding. The scent of rain hung heavy in the air, mingling with the exhaust from the bustling streets. The city pulsed with life, but for Chaya, it felt like a prison. Every footstep, every heartbeat, reminded her of the looming trial her brother faced, and the shame Mahendra had thrust upon their family. Kumar had always been her shield, her quiet protector after their father passed away. Now he was the one who needed saving, and for the first time, Chaya was the one standing between her family and ruin.

She pulled her shawl closer, wrapping it tightly around her shoulders, as she navigated the narrow alleys toward Ramachandra Shastry's office. The modest building stood in a quieter part of the city. It was modest yet dignified, much like the man she hoped to meet. Shastry's reputation preceded him. He had gained a reputation as a fighter, someone willing to challenge the system, a beacon of hope for those pushed to the brink.

She stopped outside the office door, a modest wooden sign reading "Shastry Law Associates" catching her eye.

Her hands shook as she took a deep breath and knocked, the weight of her family's fate pressing down on her shoulders.

The door opened to reveal Shastry himself, dressed in a crisp white shirt, his eyes alight with an energy that seemed out of place for such a young man. His features were sharp, his hair neatly combed, but it was his eyes that struck her—a piercing, unwavering gaze, as if he could see right through the pretenses people hid behind.

"Please, come in," he said, motioning her into the office with a calm yet confident nod. His office was humble but meticulously organized, with neatly stacked law books lining one wall and a small desk piled with case files.

Chaya stepped inside, her hands clutching her shawl for comfort. She felt vulnerable, as if every fear and hope she carried was laid bare under his scrutinizing gaze. They sat down across from each other, and for a brief moment, an uncomfortable silence stretched between them.

"What brings you here, Miss Chaya?" Shastry asked, his voice measured, soft but firm. She swallowed hard, fighting the lump in her throat. "It's my brother, Kumar. He's... he's in jail. He's been accused of something he didn't do. All he ever wanted was to protect me." Her voice wavered as she spoke, the words tumbling out in a rush, her fear and desperation laid bare.

Shastry leaned forward, his hands clasped on the table. "I'm listening," he said gently.

Chaya took a deep breath, recounting everything. The betrayal by Mahendra, Kumar's sacrifice, the mounting pressure from Mahendra's influential family, and the helplessness she felt as she watched her family's honor unravel. Her voice shook as she relayed every detail, but Shastry listened intently, never interrupting, his expression a mixture of empathy and focus.

When she finished, a tear slipped down her cheek, but she quickly wiped it away, ashamed to show her vulnerability. Shastry took a deep breath, his gaze unwavering. "Your brother's actions may have landed him in jail, but you were right—this isn't just about him. This is about justice, Chaya."

She looked at him, her eyes searching his face for any sign of hesitation, but all she saw was resolve. Chaya's hands fidgeted nervously in her lap as Shastry rose, retrieving a well-worn copy of the Indian Penal Code from a shelf behind his desk. He thumbed through the pages quickly, his eyes scanning the lines with a focus that was almost intense.

"We'll start with the basics. Inspector Thimmaiah has given me a few details, but we'll need to get the complete report. I want to see every piece of evidence the prosecution has," Shastry said, his voice calm yet commanding. He looked up at her, a glint of determination in his eye. "If they think they can bulldoze over your brother because of their connections, they're in for a surprise."

Chaya felt a flicker of hope flare to life, a light at the end of a long, dark tunnel. For the first time in weeks, she felt the weight on her shoulders lift, just a little. "Mr.

Shastry... can we win this? Will we be able to save Kumar and his friends?"

Shastry smiled, a confident smile that held both assurance and something else—passion. "Winning is not just about fighting in court. It's about fighting outside the courtroom as well, standing tall against threats and intimidation. I can't promise you an easy road, Chaya. But I can promise you this: I'll give this case everything I have. No one will push your brother down while I'm standing. In the fight against right and the might, the right should always win."

Chaya's voice trembled as she spoke, "Thank you, Mr. Shastry." Shastry shook his head. "There's no need for thanks, Chaya. This is what I do, and if there's one thing I've learned, it's that everyone deserves someone to fight for them and Kumar and his friends certainly do."

As she left his office that day, Chaya felt a new resolve take root in her heart. She wasn't alone in this fight. Shastry was by her side, a relentless force for justice. And with him leading the charge, she knew they had a chance—a real chance—to reclaim her family's honor and bring Kumar back home. Chaya knew very well that getting her money back from Mahendra was another issue altogether.

The courtroom was packed as the first day of Kumar's trial began. The tension in the air was palpable, with family members of both the accused and the victim seated anxiously on opposite sides. Chaya sat near the back, her hands clenched tightly in her lap, trying to remain calm. The only thing louder than the murmurs of the crowd was the echoing thud of the gavel as the judge entered the courtroom and called the proceedings to order.

Kumar sat in the dock, his expression grim, his eyes scanning the room as if searching for answers. His lawyer, Shastry, stood beside him, young but composed, ready to take on the case that had caught the attention of the northern part of the city. On the other side, stood the prosecutor, Mr. Murari, an older man with years of courtroom experience etched into his sharp, calculating features. Known for his aggressive style and unflinching determination, Murari was a formidable opponent.

The judge, Mallikarjun a stern, no-nonsense man, took his seat at the bench, drank a glass of water and surveyed the room before calling for the opening statements to begin.

Murari, dressed in a dark, impeccable suit, rose first. He strode confidently to the front of the courtroom, his eyes briefly sweeping over the litigants present in the court room, before locking onto Kumar. His voice was strong and commanding, filling the room.

"Your Honor," Murari began, turning toward the judge, "we are here today to bring to justice a man who, with his gang of criminals, mercilessly assaulted an innocent shopkeeper in broad daylight. Kumar and his associates not only vandalized Manjunatha Gowda's shop, but they brutally attacked him, leaving him severely injured and traumatized. This was no spontaneous act of anger—this was a deliberate, coordinated attack. We have witnesses, CCTV footage, and a victim who survived this heinous act. The evidence will show, without a shadow of a doubt, that Kumar and his gang are guilty of attempt to murder, dacoity, assault, and conspiracy. The motive behind the attack was that Mahendra, the son of the victim was in a relationship with the sister of the Accused Kumar and there seems to be some financial settling of scores between the two. I ask the court to consider the gravity of the crimes committed and to deliver justice swiftly and unequivocally."

Murari's words were met with nods from the prosecution's side. The atmosphere grew heavier, and Chaya's heart sank. Murari had painted Kumar as the leader of a vicious gang—a narrative that would be hard to dismantle.

Then, it was Shastry's turn.

The young lawyer stood up slowly, his demeanor calm but determined. He adjusted his black robes, taking a deep breath before stepping forward. Though he lacked Murari's years of experience, he possessed a quiet confidence that filled the room.

"Your Honor, Shastry began, his voice measured and clear." "The prosecution would have you believe that this case is simple, that the accused is guilty beyond any doubt. Your Honor, I urge you to look deeper. My client, Kumar and his associates are not monsters the prosecution paints them to be. Yes, mistakes were made. But what we will demonstrate throughout this trial is that Kumar is not the mastermind behind this crime. He is not the leader of any gang. He is a man who made poor choices under difficult circumstances. The evidence, which Mr. Murari claims is irrefutable, is not as conclusive as it may seem. There are gaps, there are inconsistencies, and there is more to the story than what has been presented so far. All we ask is for a fair trial, where all facts are considered, and justice is truly served—not by assumption, but by truth."

As Shastry spoke, the room grew quieter, the tension momentarily replaced by curiosity. His words carried a calm reason, and even the judge seemed to lean in slightly, paying closer attention. Chaya felt a small flicker of hope. Shastry was young, yes, but he was in control, and his words carried weight and resonated in the court hall.

Shastry turned slightly, glancing at Kumar, before continuing. "My client is prepared to take responsibility for his actions. But he will not take responsibility for what he did not do. Throughout this trial, we will show that the portrayal of Kumar as a dangerous criminal is a gross exaggeration, and we will prove that he does not deserve the harsh judgment the prosecution seeks."

Shastry returned to his seat, and the room buzzed with murmurs once again. The contrast between Murari's aggressive, damning opening and Shastry's composed, thoughtful defense was stark.

Judge Mallikarjun cleared his throat, bringing the room back to order. "Thank you, Mr. Murari and Mr. Shastry," he said, his voice authoritative but steady. "The Court has heard the opening statements. Given the seriousness of the charges, the accused, Kumar, is hereby remanded to judicial custody for a period of 14 days. Adjourned!"

Chaya's heart sank. She had hoped that there might be some reprieve for her brother today, but she knew this was just the beginning of a long, difficult process. Kumar was led away in handcuffs as the judge adjourned the session, announcing that the trial would resume after the 14-day remand period.

As the crowd began to disperse, Shastry turned to Chaya, his face solemn. "We'll fight this," he said, his voice low but firm. "This is just the beginning."

Chaya nodded, tears welling in her eyes. It wasn't the outcome she had prayed for, but Shastry's resolve gave her a reason to hope. She would cling to that hope in the days to come, as the trial would soon dive deeper into the complex web of accusations, evidence, and the battle for truth.

Couple of weeks later, Kumar and his gang are brought to court for their bail hearing. Ramachandra Shastry stands as their defense lawyer, confident but aware of the challenges ahead. On the opposite side, Mahendra watches from a distance, his own legal team advising him on how to stay clear of the mess.

"The charges against the defendants are serious—attempt to murder, vandalism, assault, and resisting arrest. Why should this court consider granting them bail?" Judge questioned Shastry looking over the case files.

"Your Honor, the defendants are innocent. Mahendra Gowda, who has been manipulating and defrauding my client's sister in order to gain unlawfully, has filed a false case. I believe that with proper oversight and assurances, they can be granted bail.

Injuries sustained by the victim as mentioned in the complaint and as mentioned in the MLC (Medico-Legal-Case) Report do not correspond with each other and as the report, the injuries are not serious in nature to attract offence under section 307. Moreover, there are no overt acts attributed against any of the Accused properly. Your Honor, these men have no criminal records. They are residents of Bengaluru and are willing to abide by any conditions the court imposes. Imprisoning them will cause undue suffering to their families." Shastry argued.

Prosecutor Mr.Murari was quick to respond "Your Honor, this is a clear-cut case of violent behavior. These men attacked an elderly man's business and evaded arrest. Granting them bail would be reckless. Your Honor, if released, these men may interfere with the investigation and tamper witness."

Kumar sat silently, staring at Mahendra, whose smirk was barely visible across the courtroom. The tension between them was palpable.

Judge Mallikarjun paused to consider. "Bail is the Rule and Jail is the Exception. At the same time, Bail is a privilege, not a right. However, given the defense's argument and the circumstances surrounding the case, I am willing to grant bail, but only under strict conditions. The defendants must report to the police station every 15 days and are forbidden from leaving the city. They shall appear before the IO whenever called for and shall appear before him every 15 days to mark attendance before the Police Station until filing of chargesheet. They shall not tamper with any of the witnesses."

Kumar and his gang breathed a sigh of relief, though the victory is bittersweet. Shastry turns to Kumar, giving him a stern look. "This is just the beginning. Don't do anything foolish. We still have a long way to go." Shastry quietly said to Kumar and gang

As the group leaves the courtroom, Mahendra steps outside, immediately surrounded by his legal team. Kumar catches his eye, and for a brief moment, their gazes lock. Kumar quips under his breath "This isn't over." Mahendra coldly answered "It never is."

Meanwhile Inspector Sridhar sat at his desk, reviewing the case files. Sub-Inspector Thimmaiah, approached him and handed over the latest reports. "We've got the footage from the shop cameras, sir. Kumar and his gang vandalized the place, but there's more. I did some digging—Mahendra's not as clean as he looks" informed Thimmaiah.

Sridhar leaned forward, intrigued and said "Go on." Thimmaiah looked over the files and remarked "Mahendra's been involved in a few shady deals. Small-time scams, using his father's shop as a front. He's got connections with some local politicians too. He'sslippery, sir."

Sridhar nodded, piecing the puzzle together. "So, Kumar's not the only one with something to hide. Interesting...Mahendra might have thought he could outsmart everyone, but it looks like he's got more skeletons in his closet than we thought." Sridhar stroked his chin, while formulating a plan.

Sridhar instructed Thimmaiah to file the chargesheet in the court and told "Keep digging. If we can find anything concrete that ties Mahendra to bigger crimes, we might have leverage. I want him in the station, answering questions."

AT THE COURTHOUSE

The tension in the courtroom was thick. Kumar and his gang stood behind their lawyer, Mr. Shastry, facing the judge. Across from them, Mahendra sat confidently with his own legal team, smirking as though he's already won. Judge Mallikarjun looked stern and spoke "These charges are serious—attempt to murder, vandalism, assault, and destruction of property. How does the defense plead?"

Kumar and his gang calmly answered as tutored by Shastry, "Your Honor, we plead not guilty. To avoid repayment of money, and to hide the truth, Mahendra Gowda has hoisted a false case."

"Your Honor, regardless of the emotions involved, this was a clear act of violence and conspiracy. We have witnesses and footage of Kumar and his friends damaging the shop." Murari argued.

"Enough. I'll hear from both sides in full during the trial. For now, the case is adjourned." Judge Mallikarjun rose. As the hearing ended, Chaya watched from the back of the courtroom, her heart heavy. She felt the weight of both her guilt and her growing desire to see Mahendra pay for what he had done and whispered to herself "I won't let him destroy my family."

On the next hearing date, the courtroom is packed as usual. Lawyers, litigants and observers, had gathered for what had already been an intense legal battle. Judge Mallikarjun presided over the session, his stern face looming from the elevated bench, his gavel resting on the desk, ready to restore order at any moment.

To his right, Shastry, the defense lawyer sat preparing his notes, glancing occasionally at Kumar and his gang, who sat in the dock with hardened expressions. The public prosecutor, Mr. Murari, stood tall and ready, his eyes gleaming with confidence.

Kumar shifted uneasily in his seat. His mind churned with a mix of anger and frustration. He had hoped things would have quieted down after the arrest, but instead, the pressure had mounted. The trial had started, and Sridhar was the prosecution's first witness.

A voice called out, shattering the silence. "Prosecution Witness Number One, Inspector Sridhar, please take the stand."

Sridhar rose from his seat with the same calm, deliberate demeanor that had defined his career. As he walked to the witness box, he noticed the way Kumar's eyes followed him—intense, burning with a quiet rage. But Sridhar was unshaken. He had faced men like Kumar before, men who thought they were untouchable. Today, he would show the court exactly why they weren't.

After taking the oath, Sridhar adjusted his posture, standing with the confidence of a man who knew he was right. "Inspector Sridhar," began the prosecutor, stepping forward, "could you please narrate the events that led to the arrest of the accused?"

Sridhar nodded and steadied his voice. "It began on the morning on 13th July. Manjunatha Gowda, the owner of a mobile repair shop in the market area, came into the police station with visible injuries. He was shaken, clearly in pain. His shop had been vandalized, and he had been assaulted."

The courtroom listened attentively, the details unfolding with every word Sridhar spoke. "He provided a detailed account of how Kumar and his associates—Prasad, Raghu, Partha, Krishna, and Ahmed—stormed into his shop. They vandalized the premises, destroyed property, and physically assaulted him. Manjunatha Gowda identified them by name."

Mr. Murari nodded, urging him to continue. "And what was your next course of action, Inspector?"

Sridhar's eyes flickered toward Kumar for a brief momentbefore he answered. "After hearing his statement, I immediately ordered an investigation. We reviewed CCTV footage from the surrounding area, including a camera positioned outside a nearby bank. The footage confirmed the presence of Kumar and his gang near the scene of the crime. Additionally, we found multiple witnesses—shopkeepers and bystanders—who corroborated Manjunatha Gowda's version of events."

As he spoke, Sridhar noticed the defense lawyer shifting in his seat. The defense would try to discredit the witnesses or challenge the evidence, but Sridhar wasprepared for that.

"And then?" prompted Mr. Murari.

"With the evidence in hand, we tracked the accused to a tea stall in a different part of the city. On the evening of July 14th, we conducted a raid and successfully apprehended Kumar and his associates. The operation was swift, and there were no fatalities."

The prosecutor smiled, knowing how airtight Sridhar's testimony was. "Inspector, can you confirm that the injuries sustained by Mr. Manjunatha Gowda were consistent with an assault?"

"Yes," Sridhar replied firmly. "The medical report indicated that he had several bruises and a fractured wrist, injuries consistent with being struck and shoved to the ground. His wounds matched the timeline he provided."

Kumar shifted uncomfortably, his expression hardening with each word. He had expected Sridhar's testimony to be damaging, but hearing it laid out so clearly in front of the court was worse than he'd imagined. The walls were closing in.

Mr. Murari glanced at the judge, then back to Sridhar. "No further questions, Your Honor."

The judge nodded, turning to the defense attorney. "Does the defense wish to cross-examine the witness?"

The room was hushed as Shastry rose from his seat, smooth and deliberate in his movements. Shastry, a sharp-eyed man with a reputation for clever tactics, stood slowly. He adjusted his black coat and approached Sridhar with measured steps, adjusting his glasses as he did so.

"Inspector Sridhar, you're an experienced officer, aren't you?" "Of course," smirked Sridhar. "You've handled many cases, some even more serious than this one, correct?" Shastry asked. "Absolutely. This case is no different" answered Sridhar cockily.

Shastry leaned forward, his voice steady but pointed "And you've been in courtrooms like this before, haven't you, Inspector? You understand how serious it is to provide accurate testimony under oath?"

Sridhar laughing lightly, trying to lighten the mood "Obviously. What are you trying to get at, Mr. Shastry?" The audience chuckled with him, some junior lawyers looking at Sridhar with admiration, as if he was impregnable. But Shastry remains unfazed. His voice sharpens as he drives his next question home.

"Inspector, how exactly did you record the victim's statement?" questioned Shastry.

"What kind of question is that? He came in, told us everything, and we filed the chargesheet. Routine procedure." Sridhar chuckled, dismissively.

The room rippled with laughter again, and Sridhar looks around, relishing the attention, thinking he's just humiliated the young lawyer. But Shastry didn't back down.

In a firmer tone Shastry shot an arrow "I'll ask you again, Inspector Sridhar. How did the victim, Manjunatha Gowda, communicate his statement to you?"

Sridhar's face twitched slightly, his smugness wavering. He noticed the shift in tone but still believed he was in control. Sridhar answered more defensively "Like I said, he told us everything. Verbally" Shastry immediately raised an eyebrow, and subtly smiled.

"Inspector, I put it to you that Manjunatha Gowda is deaf and dumb, and he could not have verbally narrated anything to you and you are falsifying under oath. Isn't that right?"

A wave of silence crashes over the room. All eyes shift to Sridhar. His smirk fades as the gravity of the situation settles in. His jaw tightens, his eyes darting toward Mr. Murari, who looks equally stunned.

Judge Mallikarjun leaned forward, narrowing his eyes and sternly enquired "Is this true, Inspector Sridhar? Sridhar stammered, beads of sweat forming on his forehead. He tried to salvage the situation, but his words fumbled "Your Honor, I... I... must have... misunderstood."

Shastry stepped forward, his voice carrying the weight of authority and roared! "Misunderstood? Inspector, are you telling this court that you took a detailed verbal statement from a man who physically cannot speak?"

Sridhar's eyes drop, the courtroom became deadly silent. Shastry paused, letting the full impact of his words settle into the room. The audience were frozen, fully absorbed in the young lawyer's relentless, surgical approach. Sridhar, visibly rattled, struggled to answer.

Judge Mallikarjun got furious "Perjury is a serious offense, Inspector! This court will not tolerate false testimony especially by a Police Circle Inspector." By the way where is Manjunath Gowda?

Gowda who was oblivious of all that was happening and seated in the front row was escorted before the bench. Judge was startled!!! Gowda was deaf and dumb since birth!!

Sridhar desperately tried to salvage the situation "Your Honor, it wasn't intentional. I—" Judge Mallikarjun slammed his gavel, silencing Sridhar's excuses and coldly ordered "Constable, take Inspector Sridhar into custody for perjury. This matter will be investigated and taken up after lunch."

The courtroom gasped as a constable stepped forward, with handcuffs in hand. Sridhar, his face pale, was being led away, his once-confident swagger completely shattered. The room, which had moments ago laughed at Shastry, now gazed at him with newfound respect.

The judge turned his attention to Shastry, nodding ever so slightly in acknowledgment of the lawyer's brilliance. Shastry nods, acknowledging the judge with professional composure, as the courtroom began to disperse.

Lawyers exchanged whispers about the brilliance of the young defense lawyer. Shastry's reputation grew before their very eyes. As Shastry packed his files, Chaya, who was sitting in the court hall, grinned from ear to ear.

Chaya came near Shastry and whispered "You nailed it, sir. That was incredible."

Shastry glanced at her, his expression cool, but there was a glint of satisfaction in his eyes. A relieved Kumar jumped "I can't believe it. You saved us." Shastry smiled modestly and answered it's not over yet, but we're on the right track. Justice will prevail.

Sridhar, who was now humiliated and facing the consequences of his false testimony, sought out Shastry privately in a desperate attempt to save his career. He approached him outside the courthouse. "Shastry, please, I need your help. You know how things can get messy in our line of work. Just help me this once, and I'll never cross you again" Sridhar pleaded.

Shastry looked at Sridhar for a moment, remembering how he had humiliated him in the past. A cold smile crossed his face as he delivered the same line Sridhar once used against him, a debt was being repaid. Shastry firmly responded "You do your work, Sridhar, and I'll do mine."

Sridhar realized his fate and replied "We both are the two sides of the same coin. Pls help!"

Judge Mallikarjun immediately presided over after lunch and raised his gavel, ready to send Sridhar to judicial custody for perjury. The courtroom braced itself for the order when Shastry, in a rare moment of calm empathy, stepped forward. With humility and conviction Shastry began "Your Honour, before this court takes any further action against Inspector Sridhar, I respectfully request a moment to address the court."

Judge Mallikarjun looked surprised by the request but gave Shastry a measured nod, gesturing for him to proceed "Very well, Mr. Shastry. But make it brief. The law must still be served."

Shastry turned towards the judge and the courtroom, his voice carrying the weight of his words which were steady and strong "Your Honour, today we have witnessed a failure—not just of an individual but of the system we all serve. Inspector Sridhar, a man entrusted with upholding the law, made a serious error in judgment. But before we rush to condemn him, let us remember that he is not the enemy."

Shastry's eyes moved across the courtroom, holding the attention of everyone present. Shastry argued inspirationally, "The police and lawyers, Your Honour, are two sides of the same coin. We both serve one master—the law. The police ensure that order is maintained, that the streets are safe from chaos, while we as lawyers challenge injustice within these very walls, defending the innocent and exposing corruption."

He began walking towards Sridhar, his steps deliberate, his voice filled emotionally and earnestly. "Inspector Sridhar, today we stand on opposite sides, but I recognize the weight you carry. Your role demands swift decisions, often under immense pressure. You act in the face of danger so that justice may prevail. But like all of us, you are human, and humans err. Today, you made a grave mistake."

Sridhar lowered his head, visibly moved by Shastry's words, his pride stripped away. Shastry pleaded to the judge, passionately "Your Honour, justice is not just about punishment—it is about understanding, balance, and the opportunity for redemption. Sridhar's error does not erase the years of honorable service he has given. He is not a villain; he is a man who, like all of us, faltered." Judge Mallikarjun listened intently, his face wore a mask of contemplation as Shastry continued.

"I humbly ask this court to consider leniency. Let the charges of perjury against Inspector Sridhar be dropped, not as an excuse for his misdeed, but as a chance for him to correct his course. This case should serve as a reminder to us all that justice only works when those entrusted with it work together, not against each other." Shastry argued finally.

He paused, letting the significance of his words resonate through the room and spoke softly, but with conviction "Inspector Sridhar and I may come from different sides of the law, but we share a common purpose: to ensure that truth and justice prevail. For the sake of that ideal, I appeal to this court for mercy."

Judge Mallikarjun paused for a moment and with measured authority spoke "Mr. Shastry, your words carry weight, and they resonate with this court. The law is not a tool of vengeance, but one of justice. Inspector Sridhar, your actions were indeed misguided, but the court recognizes your service and dedication over the years. In light of Mr. Shastry's appeal, and considering the larger interest of justice, I will exercise the court's discretion."

He turned to Sridhar sternly but with a hint of compassion "Inspector Sridhar, the charges of perjury will be dropped, but let this be a lesson—a reminder that the law does not tolerate carelessness, especially from those sworn to uphold it. The court expects better from you moving forward."

Sridhar, visibly relieved but humbled, nodded in understanding and softly said "Thank you, Your Honour."

As the courtroom began to settle, Sridhar approached Shastry, clearly affected by the events of the day. He stood before him, humbled by Shastry's grace. Sridhar quietly, but sincerely remarked Shastry, I... I don't know what to say. I didn't expect you to speak on my behalf. After everything... why?

Shastry smiled gently, offered his hand "Because, Inspector, we both serve the law. And the law doesn't work when we fight each other. It works when we stand together, no matter how hard that can be sometimes."

Sridhar hesitated for a moment, and then shook Shastry's hand firmly, a new respect forming between the two. Sridhar gratefully thanked Shastri and remarked "I'm sorry for everything. You're a better man than I gave you credit for" Shastry sincerely, with a knowing smile "No hard feelings, Sridhar. Just remember—next time, we're on the same side."

"I have a question though?" enquired Sridhar. How did you figure out that Manjunath Gowda was deaf and dumb? I mean, it was brilliant! You caught me completely off guard!

Shastry smiled and calmly replied "Well, it wasn't something that just happened overnight. I've been working on this case for weeks, and something always felt off about Manjunath's testimony. He never appeared in court, and the way you described the incident in the chargesheet—it just didn't add up. So, yesterday, I went to Manjunath Gowda's shop. Just wanted to get a feel for the man, you know? I dressed down, pretended to be a customer. Asked him for the price of a tempered glass for my mobile phone. I must've asked him three times, but he just kept working, ignoring me.

That's when I realized—he wasn't ignoring me, but he just couldn't hear me. I waved my hand in front of him. No response. Immediately, I realized that he was deaf and dumb. And then it hit me—how could a man who can't speak or hear give a detailed verbal statement to the police? You were completely overconfident and neither you nor your officers enquired Manjunath Gowda even once during investigation and depended totally on the story narrated by his son Mahendra, plain and simple.

Sridhar stunned and replied "And that's when you knew" Shastry noded "Exactly. That's when I knew we had them. I recorded the whole thing just in case, but the moment I stepped into that shop, I had all the proof I needed."

Shastry shared a brief moment of mutual respect, and Sridhar walked out of the courtroom feeling relieved. Shastry stood in the center of the court room, the weight of his victory and the restoration of justice settling in. The courtroom emptied, and Shastry took a deep breath, knowing his fight for justice will continue—but with newfound allies on both sides of the law.

Late at night, the time was 11:00 PM, and Shastry had just wrapped up a long, victorious day. His office, dimly lit, felt like a haven after the intensity of the courtroom. Papers were scattered around, files stacked high, but his heart was full of satisfaction. The weight of the victory filled both his heart and his pockets. In the silence of the night, he took a deep breath and poured himself a glass of Old Monk rum, mixing it with Thumbs Up and water.

On his desk were a few of small local packets of mango pickle—his favorite snack for nights like these. He sat back in his chair, the glass in one hand and the pickle in the other. As he took a sip, a rare sense of peace filled the room and he started singing a hymn he was taught in his school, in an ecstatic mood

> All things bright and beautiful,
>
> All creatures great and small,
>
> All things wise and wonderful,
>
> The Good God made them all.

> Each little flower that opens,
>
> Each little bird that sings,
>
> He made their glowing colors,
>
> He made their tiny wings.

> He gave us eyes to see them,
>
> And lips that we might tell
>
> How great is God Almighty,
>
> Who has made all things well.

He smiled to himself, feeling grateful for the unexpected turns of the day, for the victory, and for the way justice was served. He smiled softly to himself, knowing that his journey, in law was far from over. He poured himself one last peg, toasting to the night and to the victories yet to come.

www.ingramcontent.com/pod-product-compliance
Lightning Source LLC
LaVergne TN
LVHW041906070526
838199LV00051BA/2518